D0324954

SACRED READING

for Lent 2018

"*Sacred Reading for Lent* is a convenient size and affordable. We gave it to all of our parishioners. They really appreciated it and found it helped them develop a closer relationship with the Lord by doing as we are invited to during Lent—namely, to pray more intensely and listen to Jesus."

Rev. Tom Stehlik, C.M.
Pastor of St. Joseph Church
New Orleans, Louisiana

"Our parishioners have used the Sacred Reading series to grow in their understanding of scripture during these special liturgical seasons. It encourages them to pay attention to what they are thinking or feeling as they read the gospel and opens their minds and hearts to see how it speaks to them at that moment. It helps the scriptures become more alive and relevant in their everyday lives. This is something they can carry with them outside of Advent and Lent."

Mary Ann Fox
Manager of Faith Formation for Adults and
Christian Initiation and Liturgy Coordinator
Annunciation Catholic Church
Altamonte Springs, Florida

SACRED READING

for Lent 2018

Apostleship of Prayer
The Pope's Worldwide Prayer Network

Douglas Leonard

AVE MARIA PRESS AVE Notre Dame, Indiana

Founded in 1865, Ave Maria Press is a ministry of the United States Province of Holy Cross.

www.avemariapress.com

Paperback: ISBN-13 978-1-59471-775-8

E-book: ISBN-13 978-1-59471-776-5

Cover and text design by David Scholtes.

Printed and bound in the United States of America.

CONTENTS

INTRODUCTION

In the gospel, Jesus says his disciples will fast when he, the Bridegroom, is taken from them. We know that Jesus is always with us, but during the season of Lent we honor him in a special way by entering a forty-day period of prayer, fasting, and almsgiving in preparation for the celebration of the resurrection of the Lord, Easter Sunday. The season of Lent begins on Ash Wednesday, dividing the cycle of Ordinary Time in the Church year. Sundays in Lent are not counted as fast days. Fast days continue through Holy Saturday, the day before Easter. Lent officially ends on Holy Thursday, the beginning of the Easter triduum.

The number of days of Lent corresponds to the forty days Jesus prayed and fasted in the desert before beginning his earthly ministry. Lent is a time to allow God to help us become holy, to help us look to the needs of others and minister to those needs, and most of all, to grow in faith, hope, and love, for those virtues are of God, motivating and empowering us to live the Gospel.

One of the important ways Christians observe Lent is by taking up—or practicing with greater intentionality—certain devotional or prayer practices to help them prepare to celebrate the Easter feast with greater joy. Christians throughout the world are rediscovering a powerful, ancient form of prayer known as sacred reading (*lectio divina*) that invites communion with God through scripture reading and contemplation. What better way to deepen one's friendship with Jesus Christ, the Word of God, than by prayerfully encountering him in the daily gospel reading?

Sacred reading is a spiritual practice that, guided by the Holy Spirit, invites you to interact with the words of the daily gospel. As you read and pray this way, you may find—as many others have—that the Lord speaks to you in intimate and surprising ways. The reason for this is simple: as we open our hearts to Jesus, he opens his heart to us.

St. Paul prays beautifully for his readers:

> For this reason I bow my knees before the Father, from whom every family in heaven and on earth takes its name. I pray that, according to the riches of his glory, he may grant that you may be strengthened in your inner being with power through his Spirit, and that Christ may dwell in your hearts through faith, as you are being rooted and grounded in love. I pray that you may have the power to comprehend, with all the saints, what is the breadth and length and height and depth, and to know the love of Christ that surpasses knowledge, so that you may be filled with all the fullness of God. (Eph 3:14–19)

This book moves you through each day's gospel by prompting you at each step of lectio divina, getting you started with reading, observing, praying, listening, and resolving to act. But most important is your own response to the Word and the Spirit for that is how you will grow in your relationship with Jesus. If you are sincerely seeking God, the Holy Spirit will lead you in this process.

How to Use This Book

This book will set you on a personal prayer journey with Jesus from Ash Wednesday through the end of Holy Week. Please note that some of the readings in this booklet have been shortened for group use. The citation for shortened readings will first show the reading that is included in the book and will then show the citation for the day's complete reading in parentheses.

In prayerful reading of the daily gospels, you join your prayers with those of believers all over the world. Following the readings for Lent, you will be invited to reflect on the gospel text for the day in six simple but profound steps:

1. Know that God is present with you and ready to converse.

At all times God is everywhere, including where you are in this very moment. The human mind is incapable of fully grasping the mystery of God, but we do know some things about God from scripture. God is the transcendent ground of all being, invisible, eternal, and infinite in power. God is Love, with infinite love for you and me. God is one with and revealed through the Word, Jesus Christ, who became flesh. Through him all things were made, and by him and for him all things subsist. Jesus is the Way, the Truth, and the Life. He says that those who know him also know his Father. Through the passion, death, and resurrection of Jesus, we are reconciled with God. If we believe in Jesus Christ, we become the sons and daughters of Almighty God.

God gives us the Holy Spirit to lead us to truth and understanding. The Holy Spirit also gives us power to live obedient to the teachings of Jesus. The Holy Spirit draws us to prayer and works in us as we pray. No wonder we come into God's presence with gladness. All God's ways are good and beautiful. We can get to know God better by encountering God in the Word, which is Jesus himself.

The prompt prayer at the beginning of each day's reading is just that: a prompt, something to get you started. In fact, all the elements in the process of sacred reading are meant to prompt you to your own conversations with God. After reading the prompt, feel free to continue to pray in your own words: respond in your own way, pray in your own way, and hear God speaking to you personally. Your goal is to make sacred reading your own prayer time each day.

2. Read the Gospel.

The entire Bible is the Word of God, but the gospels (Matthew, Mark, Luke, and John) specifically tell the good news about Jesus Christ. Throughout the Church year, the daily gospel readings during Mass will come from all four gospels. The Sacred Reading series (the prayer books as well as the seasonal booklets for Advent/Christmas and Lent/Easter) concentrates on praying with the daily gospels. These readings contain the story of Jesus' life, his teachings, his works, his passion and death on the Cross, his resurrection on the third day, and his ascension into heaven.

The gospels interpret Jesus' ministry for us. Much more, by the Holy Spirit, we can find in the gospels the very person of Jesus Christ. Prayerful reading of the daily gospel is an opportunity to draw close to the Lord: Father, Son, and Holy Spirit. As we pray with the gospels, we can be transformed by the grace of God—enlightened, strengthened, and moved. Seek to read the gospel with a complete openness to what God is saying to you. Many who pray with the gospel recommend rereading it several times.

3. Notice what you think and feel as you read the gospel.

Sacred reading can involve every faculty—mind, heart, emotions, soul, spirit, sensations, imagination, and much more—though usually not all at once. Different passages touch different keys in us. Sometimes we may laugh. Sometimes we may need to stop and worship before we continue. Sometimes we will be puzzled, amazed, stung, abashed, reminded of something lovely, or reminded of something we had wanted to forget.

Seek to feel all of your emotions as you read. Apply your intellect, too. You will confront problems of context and exegesis on a daily basis. That's okay. Sometimes you may experience very little. That's okay, too. God is at work anyway. Give yourself to the gospel and take from it what is there for you each day.

Most important, notice what in particular jumps out at you, whatever it may be. It may be a word, a phrase, a character, an image, a pattern, an emotion, a sensation—some arrow to your heart. Whatever it is, pay attention to it, because the Holy Spirit is using it to accomplish something in you.

Sometimes a particular gospel repeats during the liturgical year of the Church. To pray through the same gospel even on successive days presents no problem whatsoever to your sacred reading. St. Ignatius of Loyola, founder of the Jesuits and author of *The Spiritual Exercises*, actually recommends repeated meditation on passages of Scripture. Read in the Spirit, gospel passages have unlimited potential to reveal to us the truths we are ready to receive. For the receptive soul, the Word of God has boundless power to illuminate and transform the prayerful believer.

4. *Pray as you are led for yourself and others.*

Praying is just talking with God. Believe God hears you. Believe God will answer you. Believe God knows what you need even before you ask. Jesus says so in the gospels. So your conversation with God can go far beyond asking for things. You may thank, praise, worship, rejoice, mourn, explain, question, reveal your fears, seek understanding, or ask forgiveness. Your conversation with God has no limits. God is the ideal conversationalist. God wants to spend much time with you.

Being human, we can't help being self-absorbed, but praying is not just about our own needs. We are often moved by the gospel to pray for others. We will regularly remember our loved ones in prayer. Sometimes we will be led to pray for someone who has hurt us. At other times we will be moved to pray for a class of people in need wherever they are in the world, like persecuted Christians, refugees, the mentally ill, the rich, teachers, the unborn, or the lonely.

We may also pray with the universal Church by praying for the pope's prayer intentions. Those intentions are entrusted to the Apostleship of Prayer and are available through its web site and its annual and monthly leaflets. You may get your own copy of this year's papal prayer intentions by contacting the Apostleship of Prayer. The Apostleship is the pope's prayer group, with more than thirty-five million members worldwide. Jesus asked us to unite in prayer, promising that the Father would grant us whatever we ask in his name.

5. Listen to Jesus.

Jesus the Good Shepherd speaks to his own sheep, who hear his voice (see Jn 10:27). This listening is a most wonderful time in your sacred reading prayer experience. The italicized words in this passage are the words I felt impressed upon my heart as I prayed with these readings. I included them in order to help you to listen more actively for whatever it is the Lord might be saying to you.

Jesus speaks to all in the gospels, but in your *Sacred Reading* prayer experience he can now speak exclusively to you. If you can, write down what he says to you and reread his words during the day. Put all of Jesus' words to you in a folder or keep a spiritual notebook. Believers through the ages have recorded the words of Jesus to them, holy mystics and ordinary believers alike.

It takes faith to hear the voice of Jesus. This faith will grow as you practice listening. Ideally, we will learn to hear what Jesus is saying to us all day long, as we face difficult situations perhaps. Listening to the voice of Jesus is practicing the presence of God. As St. Paul said, "In him we live and move and have our being" (Acts 17:28).

St. Ignatius Loyola called this conversation with Jesus *colloquy*. That word simply means that two or more people are talking. St. Ignatius even urges us to include the saints in our prayer conversations. We believe in the communion of saints. If you have a patron saint, don't be afraid to talk to him or her. In her autobiography, St. Thérèse of Lisieux, who was a member of the Apostleship of Prayer, describes how she spoke often with Mary and Joseph as well as Jesus.

6. *Ask God to show you how to live today.*

Pope Benedict XVI commented that sacred reading is not complete without a call to action: something in our praying leads us to do something in our day. Perhaps we find an opportunity to serve, to love, to give, to lead, or to do something good for someone else. Perhaps we find occasion to repent, to forgive, to ask forgiveness, to make amends. Open your heart to anything God might want you to do. Try to keep the conversation with God going all day long.

Asking God to show you how to live is the last step of the *Sacred Reading* prayer time, but that doesn't mean you need to end it here. Keep it going. You may drift off in the presence of God, lose attention, or even fall asleep, but you can come back. God is always present with you, seeking to love you and to be loved. God is always seeking to lead us to green pastures. God is our strength, our rock, our ever-present help in time of trouble. God is full of mercy, ready to forgive us again and again. God sees us through very difficult times. God heals us. God gives his life to us constantly. God is our Maker, Father, Mother, Lover, Servant, Savior, and Friend. We know that from the gospel. He is an inexhaustible spring of blessing and holiness in our innermost selves. The sanctification of our souls is God's work, not our own.

As you read, ask the Holy Spirit to lead you in this process. With genuine faith, open yourself to respond to the Word and the Spirit, and your relationship with Jesus will continue to deepen and to grow just as the

infant Jesus grew within the womb of the Blessed
Mother. This in turn will lead you to share the love of
Christ with all those you encounter just as the Blessed
Mother draws all those who encounter her directly to
her Son.

Other Resources to Help You

These Sacred Reading resources, both the seasonal
books and this annual prayer book, are enriched by
the spirituality of the Apostleship of Prayer (The
Pope's Worldwide Prayer Network). Since 1844 our
mission has been to encourage Catholics to pray each
day for the good of the world, the Church, and the
prayer intentions of the Holy Father. In particular, we
encourage Christians to respond to the loving gift of
Jesus Christ by making a daily offering of themselves
each day. As we give the Lord our hearts, we ask him
to make them like his own Heart, full of love, mercy,
and peace.

These booklets may be used in small groups or as a
handy individual resource for those who want a special way to draw close to Christ during Lent. If you
enjoy these reflections and would like to continue this
prayerful reading throughout the year, pick up a copy
of the Sacred Reading annual prayer guide. You can
order one through the Apostleship of Prayer website
or through avemariapress.com.

These annual books offer a personal prayer experience that can be adapted to meet your particular needs.
For example, some choose to continue to reflect upon

each day's reading in writing, either in the book or in a separate journal or notebook, to create a record of their spiritual journey for the entire year. Others supplement their daily reading from the book with the daily videos and other online resources available through the Apostleship of Prayer website (apostleshipofprayer.org).

For more information about the Apostleship of Prayer and about the other resources we have developed to help men and women cultivate habits of daily prayer, visit our website at apostleshipofprayer.org.

I pray that this experience may help you walk closely with God every day.

Douglas Leonard, PhD
Apostleship of Prayer

WEEK OF ASH WEDNESDAY

May Lent be a beneficial time to "prune" falseness, worldliness, indifference: so as not to think that everything is fine if I am fine; so as to understand that what counts is not approval, the search for success or consensus, but the cleansing of the heart and of life; so as to find again our Christian identity, namely, the love that serves, not the selfishness that serves us.

> Pope Francis
> Ash Wednesday Mass
> February 10, 2016

Wednesday, February 14, 2018
Ash Wednesday

Know that God is
present and ready to converse.

"Lord, Lent begins. I am so glad I can begin it with you and your Word."

Read the gospel: Matthew 6:1–6, 16–18.

Jesus said, "Beware of practicing your piety before others in order to be seen by them; for then you have no reward from your Father in heaven.

"So whenever you give alms, do not sound a trumpet before you, as the hypocrites do in the synagogues and in the streets, so that they may be praised by others. Truly I tell you, they have received their reward. But when you give alms, do not let your left hand know what your right hand is doing, so that your alms may be done in secret; and your Father who sees in secret will reward you.

"And whenever you pray, do not be like the hypocrites; for they love to stand and pray in the synagogues and at the street corners, so that they may be seen by others. Truly I tell you, they have received their reward. But whenever you pray, go into your room and shut the door and pray to your Father who is in secret; and your Father who sees in secret will reward you. . . .

"And whenever you fast, do not look dismal, like the hypocrites, for they disfigure their faces so as to show others that they are fasting. Truly I tell you, they have received their reward. But when you fast, put oil on your head and wash your face, so that your fasting may be seen not by others but by your Father who is in secret; and your Father who sees in secret will reward you."

Notice what you think and feel as you read the gospel.

Jesus gives some practical spiritual advice about penance, prayer, and fasting: Do it in secret, rather than for show before others. Pray, fast, and give alms to show your repentance and draw nearer to God, and he will reward you.

Pray as you are led for yourself and others.

"I have sinned, Lord, in my thoughts, words, and deeds. As I begin this season of repentance, reveal to me hidden faults and let them be washed away by your grace. I offer this season of Lent for all those you have given me . . ." (Continue in your own words.)

Listen to Jesus.

I will stay near you and wash you, enlighten you, and strengthen you as you seek me. Continue to seek me, for seeking is finding. I want us to draw nearer to one another, beloved. What else is Jesus saying to you?

Ask God to show you how to live today.

"Lord, I will to do as you ask. Use this season of prayer, fasting, and almsgiving to strengthen my resolve and keep me faithfully returning to you. Amen."

Thursday, February 15, 2018

**Know that God is
present and ready to converse.**

"Lord, I want to follow you; I am listening to your Word."

Read the gospel: Luke 9:22–25.

Jesus said, "The Son of Man must undergo great suffering, and be rejected by the elders, chief priests, and scribes, and be killed, and on the third day be raised."

Then he said to them all, "If any want to become my followers, let them deny themselves and take up their cross daily and follow me. For those who want to save their life will lose it, and those who lose their life for my sake will save it. What does it profit them if they gain the whole world, but lose or forfeit themselves?"

**Notice what you think
and feel as you read the gospel.**

Jesus prophesies his own suffering, death, and resurrection. Could they even hear it? But he goes on to exhort those who want to follow him to take up their cross every day, not seeking to save their lives but to lose their lives for his sake. You save your life by losing it.

Pray as you are led for yourself and others.

"My Jesus, I want to follow. Let me rejoice in my cross because you have given it to me. Let me rejoice in losing my life because I will be saved in you. Even in your hard way there is love and joy . . ." (Continue in your own words.)

Listen to Jesus.

You understand that suffering can be redemptive if you follow my way. Keep the good of others in mind and the suffering will seem less. Let suffering be an opportunity to minister to others. Learn from me. What else is Jesus saying to you?

Ask God to show you how to live today.

"Lord, help me. Help me use my own suffering to alleviate the suffering of others. Amen."

Friday, February 16, 2018

Know that God is present and ready to converse.

"Jesus, Bridegroom of all who love you, thank you for inviting me into your presence."

Read the gospel: Matthew 9:14–15.

Then the disciples of John came to Jesus, saying, "Why do we and the Pharisees fast often, but your disciples do not fast?" And Jesus said to them, "The wedding guests cannot mourn as long as the bridegroom is with them, can they? The days will come when the bridegroom is taken away from them, and then they will fast."

Notice what you think and feel as you read the gospel.

Jesus is answering the reasonable question of John's disciples with a reasonable answer. How can his disciples mourn when he, the Messiah, the Lord of Love, is among them? But they will fast when Jesus, the Bridegroom, is taken away from them.

Pray as you are led for yourself and others.

"Lord, I rejoice in your presence, but show me how to fast and pray when I do not feel your presence. Let that sense of distance be your signal to me that I ought to fast and pray and seek you earnestly . . ." (Continue in your own words.)

Listen to Jesus.

I understand you, beloved, and I am pleased to grant your prayer. Reach out to me in your suffering and in your abstinence, and I will draw near you and bless you. What else is Jesus saying to you?

Ask God to show you how to live today.

"With your help, Lord, I can do as you ask. Perfect in me the disciplines that please you. Glory to your holy name! Amen."

Saturday, February 17, 2018

Know that God is present and ready to converse.

"Jesus, I hear your call. You call me to repentance. I come."

Read the gospel: Luke 5:27–32.

After this Jesus went out and saw a tax collector named Levi, sitting at the tax booth; and he said to him, "Follow me." And he got up, left everything, and followed him.

Then Levi gave a great banquet for him in his house; and there was a large crowd of tax-collectors and others sitting at the table with them. The Pharisees and their scribes were complaining to his disciples, saying, "Why do you eat and drink with tax collectors and sinners?" Jesus answered, "Those who are well have no need of a physician, but those who are sick; I have come to call not the righteous but sinners to repentance."

Notice what you think and feel as you read the gospel.

The Pharisees and scribes judge Jesus for keeping company with those on the margins of society. In fact, they judge all those invited to the banquet. Jesus explains that just as healthy people don't need a doctor, he comes not for the righteous but for sinners.

Pray as you are led for yourself and others.

"Jesus, you speak so well, and you also demonstrate your mercy to sinners. You call and befriend sinners. You are my dear friend, merciful Lord. Let me show mercy to others . . ." (Continue in your own words.)

Listen to Jesus.

It is my joy to bring the lost into my kingdom. I am continuing to do this work of my Father. Invite others, dear disciple, and I will do my work within their hearts. What else is Jesus saying to you?

Ask God to show you how to live today.

"I wish to obey you, Lord. Give me opportunity and courage to do and say what is truly profitable for others. Amen."

FIRST WEEK OF LENT

For all of us, then, the season of Lent in this Jubilee Year is a favorable time to overcome our existential alienation by listening to God's word and by practicing the works of mercy. In the corporal works of mercy we touch the flesh of Christ in our brothers and sisters who need to be fed, clothed, sheltered, visited; in the spiritual works of mercy—counsel, instruction, forgiveness, admonishment and prayer—we touch more directly our own sinfulness. The corporal and spiritual works of mercy must never be separated. By touching the flesh of the crucified Jesus in the suffering, sinners can receive the gift of realizing that they too are poor and in need. By taking this path, the "proud," the "powerful," and the "wealthy" spoken of in the Magnificat can also be embraced and undeservedly loved by the crucified Lord who died and rose for them. This love alone is the answer to that yearning for infinite happiness and love that we think we can satisfy with the idols of knowledge, power and riches.

Pope Francis
October 4, 2015

Sunday, February 18, 2018
First Sunday of Lent

Know that God is present and ready to converse.

"Jesus, your message is consistent. As I read your Word, let me hear and obey."

Read the gospel: Mark 1:12–15.

And the Spirit immediately drove Jesus out into the wilderness. He was in the wilderness for forty days, tempted by Satan; and he was with the wild beasts; and the angels waited on him.

Now after John was arrested, Jesus came to Galilee, proclaiming the good news of God, and saying, "The time is fulfilled, and the kingdom of God has come near; repent, and believe in the good news."

Notice what you think and feel as you read the gospel.

Led by the Spirit, driven by the Spirit, Jesus goes into the wilderness for forty days. There he is tempted by Satan, but the angels wait on him. Afterward, he proclaims the good news of God: the time has come, the kingdom is near, repent, and believe the good news.

Pray as you are led for yourself and others.

"Jesus, I hearken to your simplicity and the simplicity in this passage from your Word. This is also your message to me: obey the Spirit with simplicity. Lord, I offer myself to you in obedience for the good of those you have given me . . ." (Continue in your own words.)

Listen to Jesus.

It is a grace to hear and respond to the Word of God, my beloved. I wish for all to hear and respond, but many do not. So it has always been. Pray for them. What else is Jesus saying to you?

Ask God to show you how to live today.

"Lord, let me join you in the wilderness; let me be driven by the Spirit to pray often for all those who need to hear your message of salvation."

Monday, February 19, 2018

Know that God is present and ready to converse.

"Glorious Lord, all your judgments are just. Let your goodness reign in my heart, so that I may do your will."

Read the gospel: Matthew 25:31–46.

Jesus said, "When the Son of Man comes in his glory, and all the angels with him, then he will sit on the throne of his glory. All the nations will be gathered before him, and he will separate people one from another as a shepherd separates the sheep from the goats, and he will put the sheep at his right hand and the goats at the left. Then the king will say to those at his right hand, 'Come, you that are blessed by my Father, inherit the kingdom prepared for you from the foundation of the world; for I was hungry and you gave me food, I was thirsty and you gave me something to drink, I was a stranger and you welcomed me, I was naked and you gave me clothing, I was sick and you took care of me, I was in prison and you visited me.' Then the righteous will answer him, 'Lord, when was it that we saw you hungry and gave you food, or thirsty and gave you something to drink? And when was it that we saw you a stranger and welcomed you, or naked and gave you clothing? And when was it that we saw you sick or in prison and visited you?' And the king will answer them, 'Truly I tell you, just as you did it to one of the least of these who are members of my family, you did it to me.' Then he will say to those at his left hand, 'You that are accursed, depart from me into the eternal fire prepared for the devil and his angels; for I was hungry and you gave me no food, I was thirsty and you gave me nothing to drink, I was a stranger and you did not welcome me, naked and you did not give me clothing, sick and in prison and you did not visit me.' Then they also will answer, 'Lord, when was it that we saw you hungry or thirsty or a stranger or naked or sick or in prison, and did not take care of you?' Then he will answer them, 'Truly I tell you, just as you did not do it to one of the least of these, you did not do it to me.' And these will go away into eternal punishment, but the righteous into eternal life."

Notice what you think and feel as you read the gospel.

Jesus speaks of the judgment of nations and of people. Who will be sent to eternal punishment? Those who ignore the poor, the hungry, thirsty, naked, sick, or imprisoned. But those who cared for the poor and suffering and welcomed strangers will be rewarded with eternal life, for they did it unto Jesus himself.

Pray as you are led for yourself and others.

"Jesus, give me your heart of solidarity with the poor and suffering of this world and of my own community. Show me what I can do for them, for you . . ." (Continue in your own words.)

Listen to Jesus.

I will show you, my dear disciple. Do not forget your resolution to minister to me. You will come to know me well through the faces of those who suffer. Thank you. What else is Jesus saying to you?

Ask God to show you how to live today.

"Lord, I thank you for your wisdom and your love. I praise you for the opportunities you give me to do your work. Keep me mindful, help me see you in all your family members, and give me courage to serve you. Amen."

Tuesday, February 20, 2018

Know that God is present and ready to converse.

"Heavenly Father, your Son opened the way to you and gave me the privilege to speak to you as a Father. I do so today as I read your Word."

Read the gospel: Matthew 6:7–15.

Jesus said, "When you are praying, do not heap up empty phrases as the Gentiles do; for they think that they will be heard because of their many words. Do not be like them, for your Father knows what you need before you ask him.

"Pray then in this way:

Our Father in heaven,
hallowed be your name.
Your kingdom come.
Your will be done,
on earth as it is in heaven.
Give us this day our daily bread.
And forgive us our debts,
as we also have forgiven our debtors.
And do not bring us to the time of trial,
but rescue us from the evil one.

For if you forgive others their trespasses, your heavenly Father will also forgive you; but if you do not forgive others, neither will your Father forgive your trespasses."

Notice what you think and feel as you read the gospel.

Jesus teaches his disciples to pray to his Father in this beautiful, profound prayer. There is much he could have said to explain every phrase, but he chooses to explain the words about forgiveness—that we are forgiven by God as we forgive others. He clearly wants to emphasize that.

Pray as you are led for yourself and others.

"Lord, whom have I not forgiven? Do I hold grudges in any relationship, old or new? Let me now forgive all those who have trespassed against me . . ." (Continue in your own words.)

Listen to Jesus.

And I forgive you, my child. Do not be afraid to face your sins and repent. That is pleasing to God. It lets you draw near to God's holy self. You are a beloved child of God. What else is Jesus saying to you?

Ask God to show you how to live today.

"Thank you for your grace, dear Lord. Let me be quick to forgive others today. Amen."

Wednesday, February 21, 2018

Know that God is
present and ready to converse.

"Lord, I rejoice that you are here with me. Open me to understand your Word as you would have me understand it."

Read the gospel: Luke 11:29–32.

When the crowds were increasing, Jesus began to say, "This generation is an evil generation; it asks for a sign, but no sign will be given to it except the sign of Jonah. For just as Jonah became a sign to the people of Nineveh, so the Son of Man will be to this generation. The queen of the South will rise at the judgement with the people of this generation and condemn them, because she came from the ends of the earth to listen to the wisdom of Solomon, and see, something greater than Solomon is here! The people of Nineveh will rise up at the judgement with this generation and condemn it, because they repented at the proclamation of Jonah, and see, something greater than Jonah is here!"

Notice what you think
and feel as you read the gospel.

Jesus does not curry favor or flatter his hearers. He speaks prophetically of judgment and lets them know he is greater than Jonah or Solomon. Yet, he says, they continue to seek a sign and will not repent.

Pray as you are led for yourself and others.

"Lord, I repent, I believe your words, and I pray with all my heart for those of this generation who refuse you . . ." (Continue in your own words.)

Listen to Jesus.

Many reject me, but many respond. I am glad you do not give up on those who resist my grace. Show them love and mercy, for I do not wish them to be lost. Your sincere love has power to draw them to me, my dearest one. What else is Jesus saying to you?

Ask God to show you how to live today.

"Lord, help me practice love and mercy today, that my actions may be a sign of your great love and salvation. Amen."

Thursday, February 22, 2018
Chair of Saint Peter, Apostle

Know that God is present and ready to converse.

"Father, you enlighten the minds of your people and give them power to do your will. Let me be enlightened and empowered by your holy Word."

Read the gospel: Matthew 16:13–19.

Now when Jesus came into the district of Caesarea Philippi, he asked his disciples, "Who do people say that the Son of Man is?" And they said, "Some say John the Baptist, but others Elijah, and still others Jeremiah or one of the prophets." He said to them, "But who do you say that I am?" Simon Peter answered, "You are the Messiah, the Son of the living God." And Jesus answered him, "Blessed are you, Simon son of Jonah! For flesh and blood has not revealed this to you, but my Father in heaven. And I tell you, you are Peter, and on this rock I will build my church, and the gates of Hades will not prevail against it. I will give you the keys of the kingdom of heaven, and whatever you bind on earth will be bound in heaven, and whatever you loose on earth will be loosed in heaven."

Notice what you think and feel as you read the gospel.

Jesus knows that many misunderstand his identity, so he questions his disciples. Peter answers, saying that Jesus is the Messiah, the Son of the living God. Jesus does not deny it but instead lets Peter and the other disciples know that Peter's answer was inspired by God and declares that he will build his church upon Peter and give him authority in heaven and on earth.

Pray as you are led for yourself and others.

"Jesus, Son of the living God, I give myself to you for any purpose or use whatsoever. I give myself for the good of all those you wish me to serve, including . . ." (Continue in your own words.)

Listen to Jesus.

The Spirit of God moves through the Church, and, though assaulted by people and by Satan, the Church will not fail. Do what you can to restore integrity among believers, for some grow cold and serve themselves, not others. What else is Jesus saying to you?

Ask God to show you how to live today.

"Lord, I would honor your presence in the Church and in myself. Let me speak of your goodness and faithfulness. Amen."

Friday, February 23, 2018

Know that God is present and ready to converse.

"Lord, I praise and worship you. Allow me to follow your teachings."

Read the gospel: Matthew 5:20–26.

Jesus said, "For I tell you, unless your righteousness exceeds that of the scribes and Pharisees, you will never enter the kingdom of heaven.

"You have heard that it was said to those of ancient times, 'You shall not murder'; and 'whoever murders shall be liable to judgement.' But I say to you that if you are angry with a brother or sister, you will be liable to judgement; and if you insult a brother or sister, you will be liable to the council; and if you say, 'You fool,' you will be liable to the hell of fire. So when you are offering your gift at the altar, if you remember that your brother or sister has something against you, leave your gift there before the altar and go; first be reconciled to your brother or sister, and then come and offer your gift. Come to terms quickly with your accuser while you are on the way to court with him, or your accuser may hand you over to the judge, and the judge to the guard, and you will be thrown into prison. Truly I tell you, you will never get out until you have paid the last penny."

Notice what you think and feel as you read the gospel.

Jesus insists on true righteousness among his followers, for without it, they will never enter the kingdom of heaven. He speaks of the commandment "You shall not murder" explaining murder as any anger or insult against another. He urges us to apologize to those we have offended and to reconcile with our accusers so that we may not be judged guilty of murder.

Pray as you are led for yourself and others.

"Lord, let me appreciate the seriousness of your words, so that I will take them to heart and obey them. To whom do I owe an apology? With whom do I need to seek reconciliation? . . ." (Continue in your own words.)

Listen to Jesus.

Let your righteousness be humility, and your only virtue, my mercy. Abide with me—talk with me, walk with me— and I will show you the way, I will teach you the truth, and I will give you life. What else is Jesus saying to you?

Ask God to show you how to live today.

"Lord, walk with me in every moment of the day; help me turn to you when I feel anger, and give me your grace that I may respond to offenses with love and humility. Amen."

Saturday, February 24, 2018

Know that God is present and ready to converse.

"Merciful Father, send your Spirit into my heart as I contemplate your Word."

Read the gospel: Matthew 5:43–48.

Jesus said, "You have heard that it was said, 'You shall love your neighbor and hate your enemy.' But I say to you, Love your enemies and pray for those who persecute you, so that you may be children of your Father in heaven; for he makes his sun rise on the evil and on the good, and sends rain on the righteous and on the unrighteous. For if you love those who love you, what reward do you have? Do not even the tax collectors do the same? And if you greet only your brothers and sisters, what more are you doing than others? Do not even the Gentiles do the same? Be perfect, therefore, as your heavenly Father is perfect."

Notice what you think and feel as you read the gospel.

To love those who hate us is godly, says Jesus, even if they persecute and kill you. That is what it is to be perfect, like God our heavenly Father.

Pray as you are led for yourself and others.

"Lord, you make it so simple but so hard. I need your grace to love, truly love, those who hate me and hurt me. I offer myself to you. Conform me to your image, Jesus . . ." (Continue in your own words.)

Listen to Jesus.

Child of our Father, you will find great power and peace in loving others, both those who love you and those who hate you. Lean on me, and you shall succeed. What else is Jesus saying to you?

Ask God to show you how to live today.

"Lord, let me encounter someone who hates me, dislikes me, or is rude to me, and let me truly love him or her. I seek to obey you, Master. Amen."

SECOND WEEK OF LENT

God's way of acting may seem so far removed from our own, that he was annihilated for our sake, while it seems difficult for us to even forget ourselves a little. He comes to save us; we are called to choose his way: the way of service, of giving, of forgetfulness of ourselves.

Pope Francis
March 20, 2016

Sunday, February 25, 2018
Second Sunday of Lent

Know that God is
present and ready to converse.

"Father of Light, speak to me today by your Word."

Read the gospel: Mark 9:2–10.

Six days later, Jesus took with him Peter and James and John, and led them up a high mountain apart, by themselves. And he was transfigured before them, and his clothes became dazzling white, such as no one on earth could bleach them. And there appeared to them Elijah with Moses, who were talking with Jesus. Then Peter said to Jesus, "Rabbi, it is good for us to be here; let us make three dwellings, one for you, one for Moses, and one for Elijah." He did not know what to say, for they were terrified. Then a cloud overshadowed them, and from the cloud there came a voice, "This is my Son, the Beloved; listen to him!" Suddenly when they looked around, they saw no one with them any more, but only Jesus.

As they were coming down the mountain, he ordered them to tell no one about what they had seen, until after the Son of Man had risen from the dead. So they kept the matter to themselves, questioning what this rising from the dead could mean.

Notice what you think and feel as you read the gospel.

Three of his disciples are present on the mountain when Jesus is transfigured. Even his clothes turn bright white. Elijah and Moses appear and talk with Jesus. Peter doesn't know what to do, and God himself provides Peter with the answer: "This is my Son, the Beloved; listen to him." Jesus tells them to keep this incident secret until after his has risen, and the disciples are left to wonder what that means.

Pray as you are led for yourself and others.

"Lord, I am sure that I am just as clueless as you move and work around me. Open my ears to listen to you, and open my eyes to your glory. Help me to pray for those you have given me . . ." (Continue in your own words.)

Listen to Jesus.

I love you as my Father loves me, and the Father's love is my glory. Make a dwelling for me in your heart, beloved; abide in this tremendous love and enfold others as you go. What else is Jesus saying to you?

Ask God to show you how to live today.

"School me in love, Lord—I am listening. Let me receive it, and let me give it—the pure love of God. Amen."

Monday, February 26, 2018

Know that God is present and ready to converse.

"Lord, teach me obedience to your law. Light my path with your holy Word."

Read the gospel: Luke 6:36–38.

Jesus said, "Be merciful, just as your Father is merciful.

"Do not judge, and you will not be judged; do not condemn, and you will not be condemned. Forgive, and you will be forgiven; give, and it will be given to you. A good measure, pressed down, shaken together, running over, will be put into your lap; for the measure you give will be the measure you get back."

Notice what you think and feel as you read the gospel.

Be merciful, don't judge, forgive, and give—that's what the Lord asks of us, and he will reward us proportionately to our generosity.

Pray as you are led for yourself and others.

"Sometimes I hold back mercy, forgiveness, generosity, Lord, because I am afraid and selfish. Breathe upon me with your Spirit, and blow away my fears and selfishness. Make me a worthy child of the Father, as you are. Do this not just for me but for those I pray for now . . ." (Continue in your own words.)

Listen to Jesus.

Holiness is simple, my child. It is what I will for you, for I wish you blessing and joy. I understand you need to die to yourself to become holy. Join yourself to the Crucified. What else is Jesus saying to you?

Ask God to show you how to live today.

"Lord, thank you for dying for me. Show me how to die to myself today. How can dying to myself become second nature for me? Amen."

Tuesday, February 27, 2018

Know that God is present and ready to converse.

"Lord, I rejoice in your presence here with me now. You must have something to tell me by your Word. I praise you!"

Read the gospel: Matthew 23:1–12.

Then Jesus said to the crowds and to his disciples, "The scribes and the Pharisees sit on Moses' seat; therefore, do whatever they teach you and follow it; but do not do as they do, for they do not practice what they teach. They tie up heavy burdens, hard to bear, and lay them on the shoulders of others; but they themselves are unwilling to lift a finger to move them. They do all their deeds to be seen by others; for they make their phylacteries broad and their fringes long. They love to have the place of honor at banquets and the best seats in the synagogues, and to be greeted with respect in the marketplaces, and to have people call them rabbi. But you are not to be called rabbi, for you have one teacher, and you are all students. And call no one your father on earth, for you have one Father—the one in heaven. Nor are you to be called instructors, for you have one instructor, the Messiah. The greatest among you will be your servant. All who exalt themselves will be humbled, and all who humble themselves will be exalted."

Notice what you think and feel as you read the gospel.

Jesus exhorts the crowds and his disciples not to live religiously to please or impress others. They are not our teachers; only God is. We are students, learning humility before others and before God.

Pray as you are led for yourself and others.

"Mighty Messiah, Son of the Father, instruct me in your ways, that I may draw my life from God alone, not from others. I give to you all those I love, that you may be their teacher, too . . ." (Continue in your own words.)

Listen to Jesus.

Beloved, return to me often; come as a student, as a child. Hold every circumstance up into my light, and I will guide you. What else is Jesus saying to you?

Ask God to show you how to live today.

"What a privilege to have constant access to God, my Jesus. Help me turn to the Father today, again and again, with joyful humility. Amen."

Wednesday, February 28, 2018

Know that God is present and ready to converse.

"Lord, I seek you, and here you are. Glory to your name, O Lord."

Read the gospel: Matthew 20:17–28.

While Jesus was going up to Jerusalem, he took the twelve disciples aside by themselves, and said to them on the way, "See, we are going up to Jerusalem, and the Son of Man will be handed over to the chief priests and scribes, and they will condemn him to death; then they will hand him over to the Gentiles to be mocked and flogged and crucified; and on the third day he will be raised."

Then the mother of the sons of Zebedee came to him with her sons, and kneeling before him, she asked a favor of him. And he said to her, "What do you want?" She said to him, "Declare that these two sons of mine will sit, one at your right hand and one at your left, in your kingdom." But Jesus answered, "You do not know what you are asking. Are you able to drink the cup that I am about to drink?" They said to him, "We are able." He said to them, "You will indeed drink my cup, but to sit at my right hand and at my left, this is not mine to grant, but it is for those for whom it has been prepared by my Father."

When the ten heard it, they were angry with the two brothers. But Jesus called them to him and said, "You know that the rulers of the Gentiles lord it over them, and their great ones are tyrants over them. It will not be so among you; but whoever wishes to be great among you must be your servant, and whoever wishes to be first among you must be your slave; just as the Son of Man came not to be served but to serve, and to give his life a ransom for many."

Notice what you think and feel as you read the gospel.

Jesus predicts his Passion, Death, and Resurrection, but the apostles don't seem to hear it. The mother of the sons of Zebedee, however, has great ambition for her sons, that they may be powerful and honored in the kingdom. Jesus tells them that they don't know what they are asking, for they must drink the cup he will drink. They say they can, and he says they will.

Pray as you are led for yourself and others.

"Lord, you give me your cup to drink, too. Because of you, I can and will drink it. Let me accompany you in the way of the Cross, truly understanding the meaning of it. I offer my suffering for others . . ." (Continue in your own words.)

Listen to Jesus.

The night passes. Hard times give way to joy. Shake off mourning and look to me, for you shall be like me, robed in glory. The night is short. What else is Jesus saying to you?

Ask God to show you how to live today.

"Lord, help me understand that the end of things gives meaning to the day by day proceedings of my life. Let me keep my eyes on the prize: you. Amen."

Thursday, March 1, 2018

Know that God is present and ready to converse.

"I am your student, Jesus, Messiah. What do you have to say to me?"

Read the gospel: Luke 16:19–31.

Jesus said, "There was a rich man who was dressed in purple and fine linen and who feasted sumptuously every day. And at his gate lay a poor man named Lazarus, covered with sores, who longed to satisfy his hunger with what fell from the rich man's table; even the dogs would come and lick his sores. The poor man died and was carried away by the angels to be with Abraham. The rich man also died and was buried. In Hades, where he was being tormented, he looked up and saw Abraham far away with Lazarus by his side. He called out, 'Father Abraham, have mercy on me, and send Lazarus to dip the tip of his finger in water and cool my tongue; for I am in agony in these flames.' But Abraham said, 'Child, remember that during your lifetime you received your good things, and Lazarus in like manner evil things; but now he is comforted here, and you are in agony. Besides all this, between you and us a great chasm has been fixed, so that those who might want to pass from here to you cannot do so, and no one can cross from there to us.' He said, 'Then, father, I beg you to send him to my father's house—for I have five brothers—that he may warn them, so that they will not also come into this place of torment.' Abraham replied, 'They have Moses and the prophets; they should listen to them.' He said, 'No, father Abraham; but if someone goes to them from the dead, they will repent.' He said to him, 'If they do not listen to Moses and the prophets, neither will they be convinced even if someone rises from the dead.'"

Notice what you think and feel as you read the gospel.

Circumstances in our lives do not necessarily correspond to what we deserve. But we all have opportunities to do good to those in need. The rich man does not do good to poor, sick Lazarus, who dies and goes to heaven. The rich man dies and is tormented in Hades, where he begs for water, but Abraham says what he and Lazarus are receiving now is just. The rich man begs Abraham to send Lazarus back to his father's house to warn his brothers of the torment. Abraham says it would do no good: they won't believe it even if someone rises from the dead.

Pray as you are led for yourself and others.

"How true this parable is, my Jesus. People do not hear your words of truth, nor believe you rose from the dead. I believe, Lord. I pray now for all those who do not believe. Open their hearts . . ." (Continue in your own words.)

Listen to Jesus.

Every day the glory of God is on display, my child. Attune your heart to God's glory. As you do that, others will see it and follow. What else is Jesus saying to you?

Ask God to show you how to live today.

"Lord, Creator of the universe, let me glimpse your glory today and worship you with my whole heart, mind, soul, and strength. Amen."

Friday, March 2, 2018

Know that God is present and ready to converse.

"Lord, your ways are high above our ways. I open my heart to the truth of your Word."

Read the gospel: Matthew 21:33–43, 45–46.

Jesus said, "Listen to another parable. There was a landowner who planted a vineyard, put a fence around

it, dug a wine press in it, and built a watchtower. Then
he leased it to tenants and went to another country.
When the harvest time had come, he sent his slaves
to the tenants to collect his produce. But the tenants
seized his slaves and beat one, killed another, and
stoned another. Again he sent other slaves, more than
the first; and they treated them in the same way. Finally
he sent his son to them, saying, 'They will respect my
son.' But when the tenants saw the son, they said to
themselves, 'This is the heir; come, let us kill him and
get his inheritance.' So they seized him, threw him out
of the vineyard, and killed him. Now when the owner
of the vineyard comes, what will he do to those tenants?" They said to him, "He will put those wretches
to a miserable death, and lease the vineyard to other
tenants who will give him the produce at the harvest
time."

Jesus said to them, "Have you never read in the
scriptures:

'The stone that the builders rejected
    has become the cornerstone;
this was the Lord's doing,
    and it is amazing in our eyes'?

Therefore I tell you, the kingdom of God will be taken
away from you and given to a people that produces
the fruits of the kingdom." . . .

When the chief priests and the Pharisees heard his
parables, they realized that he was speaking about
them. They wanted to arrest him, but they feared the
crowds, because they regarded him as a prophet.

Notice what you think and feel as you read the gospel.

Jesus' prophetic parable falls on hard hearts. He compares the religious leaders of his time to tenants who beat and kill all those sent to them by the owner of the vineyard, including the owner's son. Even the priests and Pharisees declare the tenants deserve death. Jesus quotes the scripture passage about the rejected stone that becomes the cornerstone, a metaphor for himself. The religious leaders resent him but are afraid to arrest him because of the crowds who believe in him.

Pray as you are led for yourself and others.

"Lord, your awareness of past, present, and future is whole and true. I cannot see my way ahead. Would you lead me? And will you guide all those you have given me in the ways that they should go? . . ." (Continue in your own words.)

Listen to Jesus.

I am with you, beloved servant, my friend. Your love for others comes from me. You are producing the fruit of the harvest, love. Give it to me, and I will give it back to you abundantly, and it will flow out upon others. What else is Jesus saying to you?

Ask God to show you how to live today.

"I do give you my love. You, rejected, broken, and glorified, are my cornerstone. Let me be amazed by you all day long. Amen."

Saturday, March 3, 2018

Know that God is
present and ready to converse.

"Jesus, thank you for coming to me. Do you have a story that will ring true in my heart and change my life? Let me receive your Word, Lord."

Read the gospel: Luke 15:1–3, 11–32.

Now all the tax collectors and sinners were coming near to listen to Jesus. And the Pharisees and the scribes were grumbling and saying, "This fellow welcomes sinners and eats with them." . . .

Then Jesus said, "There was a man who had two sons. The younger of them said to his father, 'Father, give me the share of the property that will belong to me.' So he divided his property between them. A few days later the younger son gathered all he had and travelled to a distant country, and there he squandered his property in dissolute living. When he had spent everything, a severe famine took place throughout that country, and he began to be in need. So he went and hired himself out to one of the citizens of that country, who sent him to his fields to feed the pigs. He would gladly have filled himself with the pods that the pigs were eating; and no one gave him anything. But when he came to himself he said, 'How many of my father's hired hands have bread enough and to spare, but here I am dying of hunger! I will get up and go to my father, and I will say to him, "Father, I have sinned against heaven and before you; I am no longer worthy to be called your son; treat me like one of your hired hands.'" So he set off and went to his father. But while he was still far off, his father saw him and was filled with compassion; he ran and put his arms around him and kissed him. Then the son said to him, 'Father, I have sinned against heaven and before you; I am no longer worthy to be called your son.' But the father said to his slaves, 'Quickly, bring out a robe—the best one—and put it on him; put a ring on his finger and sandals on his feet. And get the fatted calf and kill it, and let us eat and celebrate; for this son of mine was dead and is alive again; he was lost and is found!' And they began to celebrate.

"Now his elder son was in the field; and when he came and approached the house, he heard music and dancing. He called one of the slaves and asked what was going on. He replied, 'Your brother has come, and your father has killed the fatted calf, because he has got him back safe and sound.' Then he became angry and refused to go in. His father came out and began to plead with him. But he answered his father, 'Listen! For all these years I have been working like a slave for you, and I have never disobeyed your command; yet you have never given me even a young goat so that I might celebrate with my friends. But when this son of yours came back, who has devoured your property with prostitutes, you killed the fatted calf for him!' Then the father said to him, 'Son, you are always with me, and all that is mine is yours. But we had to celebrate and rejoice, because this brother of yours was dead and has come to life; he was lost and has been found.'"

Notice what you think and feel as you read the gospel.

This parable extolls the mercy of God, who, like Jesus, welcomes the sinner who returns to him. The father is overjoyed at the return of the wayward son, making the dutiful son angry and jealous, but the father consoles him, too. His mercy is for all.

Pray as you are led for yourself and others.

"Thank you for having mercy upon me, Lord. I see myself in both sons, but more important, I see your mercy toward me. Together let us extend it to all we encounter today . . ." (Continue in your own words.)

Listen to Jesus.

No matter where you wander, you can always come home to me, dear one. I will welcome you with joy and bless you with eternal life. Pray for those who have walked away from God. What else is Jesus saying to you?

Ask God to show you how to live today.

"I offer you my day, Lord, my thoughts, words, deeds, joys, and suffering, as a prayer for all those you have given me and all those I encounter in my day. Amen."

THIRD WEEK OF LENT

The happiness that everyone desires, for that matter, can be expressed in any number of ways and attained only if we are capable of loving. This is the way. It is always a matter of love; there is no other path.

Pope Francis
June 12, 2016

Sunday, March 4, 2018
Third Sunday of Lent

Know that God is
present and ready to converse.

"Lord, I am not worthy that you should come to me
and speak to me through your Spirit and your Word.
I will hear you now."

Read the gospel: John 2:13–25.

The Passover of the Jews was near, and Jesus went up
to Jerusalem. In the temple he found people selling cattle, sheep, and doves, and the money changers seated
at their tables. Making a whip of cords, he drove all of
them out of the temple, both the sheep and the cattle.
He also poured out the coins of the money changers
and overturned their tables. He told those who were
selling the doves, "Take these things out of here! Stop
making my Father's house a marketplace!" His disciples remembered that it was written, "Zeal for your
house will consume me." The Jews then said to him,
"What sign can you show us for doing this?" Jesus
answered them, "Destroy this temple, and in three
days I will raise it up." The Jews then said, "This temple has been under construction for forty-six years, and
will you raise it up in three days?" But he was speaking
of the temple of his body. After he was raised from the
dead, his disciples remembered that he had said this;
and they believed the scripture and the word that Jesus
had spoken.

When he was in Jerusalem during the Passover festival, many believed in his name because they saw the signs that he was doing. But Jesus on his part would not entrust himself to them, because he knew all people and needed no one to testify about anyone; for he himself knew what was in everyone.

Notice what you think and feel as you read the gospel.

Jesus is angered by those seeking to profit in the Temple, for it is his Father's house. He then prophesies the destruction of the Temple, while referring at the same time to his own death and resurrection on the third day. Many people came to believe in him because of the miracles he performed, but Jesus knew their hearts had not been won over.

Pray as you are led for yourself and others.

"Lord, I seek to worship the Father in spirit and in truth. Purge all worldliness from my soul. Call me to true holiness now, and call those you have given me . . ." (Continue in your own words.)

Listen to Jesus.

You have come to me and tasted my love and wisdom, beloved. I give them to you gladly. You comfort me with your love and earnestness to please me. You do please me, beloved. What else is Jesus saying to you?

Ask God to show you how to live today.

"Teach me to remain in your love in all the circumstances of my days, starting with this day. Lord, walk with me. Amen."

Monday, March 5, 2018

**Know that God is
present and ready to converse.**

"Jesus, sometimes you speak sternly. If you speak sternly to me, let me truly hear you and learn from you."

Read the gospel: Luke 4:24–30.

And Jesus said, "Truly I tell you, no prophet is accepted in the prophet's home town. But the truth is, there were many widows in Israel in the time of Elijah, when the heaven was shut up for three years and six months, and there was a severe famine over all the land; yet Elijah was sent to none of them except to a widow at Zarephath in Sidon. There were also many lepers in Israel in the time of the prophet Elisha, and none of them was cleansed except Naaman the Syrian." When they heard this, all in the synagogue were filled with rage. They got up, drove him out of the town, and led him to the brow of the hill on which their town was built, so that they might hurl him off the cliff. But he passed through the midst of them and went on his way.

Notice what you think and feel as you read the gospel.

The people in the synagogue in Jesus' hometown do not accept him, even as a prophet. They are angry to the point of wanting to kill him, but he slips away. His time has not yet come.

Pray as you are led for yourself and others.

"I pray for all those who are angry with God. Let this be their time of mercy, Lord. And if I have anger in my heart toward you or any person, help me forgive, and please transform that anger into love . . ." (Continue in your own words.)

Listen to Jesus.

The Spirit dwells within you, beloved, enlightening you and changing you. Give yourself to this process, knowing it is not your work but mine. Trust me. What else is Jesus saying to you?

Ask God to show you how to live today.

"Lord, I want to do my part, but you seem to be telling me to let you do yours. It is my part to let go and trust you. Amen."

Tuesday, March 6, 2018

Know that God is
present and ready to converse.

"Lord, the universe is full of beings, laws, forces, and spirits. What is important for me?"

Read the gospel: Matthew 18:21–35.

Then Peter came and said to Jesus, "Lord, if another member of the church sins against me, how often should I forgive? As many as seven times?" Jesus said to him, "Not seven times, but, I tell you, seventy-seven times.

"For this reason the kingdom of heaven may be compared to a king who wished to settle accounts with his slaves. When he began the reckoning, one who owed him ten thousand talents was brought to him; and, as he could not pay, his lord ordered him to be sold, together with his wife and children and all his possessions, and payment to be made. So the slave fell on his knees before him, saying, 'Have patience with me, and I will pay you everything.' And out of pity for him, the lord of that slave released him and forgave him the debt. But that same slave, as he went out, came upon one of his fellow slaves who owed him a hundred denarii; and seizing him by the throat, he said, 'Pay what you owe.' Then his fellow slave fell down and pleaded with him, 'Have patience with me, and I will pay you.' But he refused; then he went and threw him into prison until he should pay the debt.

When his fellow slaves saw what had happened, they were greatly distressed, and they went and reported to their lord all that had taken place. Then his lord summoned him and said to him, 'You wicked slave! I forgave you all that debt because you pleaded with me. Should you not have had mercy on your fellow slave, as I had mercy on you?' And in anger his lord handed him over to be tortured until he should pay his entire debt. So my heavenly Father will also do to every one of you, if you do not forgive your brother or sister from your heart."

Notice what you think and feel as you read the gospel.

Peter wonders about forgiveness—how much forgiveness is appropriate? Jesus tells him he must forgive those who offend him an infinite number of times. His parable makes the point that one who is forgiven by God is in no position to withhold forgiveness from others. Those who are not merciful will be punished.

Pray as you are led for yourself and others.

"Lord, I open my heart to your mercy—to receive it and to dispense it liberally. You came to forgive sins and restore us to friendship with God. Our part is to forgive the sins of others. Let me do that now . . ." (Continue in your own words.)

Listen to Jesus.

I have made the mysteries of God understandable to you, dear child. You know what you need to know. Let it sink deeply within you and change what you think, say, and do. What else is Jesus saying to you?

Ask God to show you how to live today.

"I resolve to forgive someone today. Let me see it and do it, Lord. Amen."

Wednesday, March 7, 2018

Know that God is present and ready to converse.

"Lord, let me hear your Word today, obey, and teach it by my life."

Read the gospel: Matthew 5:17–19.

Jesus said, "Do not think that I have come to abolish the law or the prophets; I have come not to abolish but to fulfill. For truly I tell you, until heaven and earth pass away, not one letter, not one stroke of a letter, will pass from the law until all is accomplished. Therefore, whoever breaks one of the least of these commandments, and teaches others to do the same, will be called least in the kingdom of heaven; but whoever does them and teaches them will be called great in the kingdom of heaven."

Notice what you think
and feel as you read the gospel.

Jesus says he fulfills the law and the prophets. He urges obedience to all God's commandments. Those who do not will be called least in the kingdom of heaven.

Pray as you are led for yourself and others.

"Lord, do I obey all your commandments? Do I minimize for myself and others the importance of obedience? Forgive me. Rescue me. Teach me to obey . . ." (Continue in your own words.)

Listen to Jesus.

My Father seeks to make you holy, perfectly holy, because that is what will make you happy, now and forever. Would you give yourself to God for that, beloved disciple? What else is Jesus saying to you?

Ask God to show you how to live today.

"I do give myself to you, Lord. Let it be for my good and the good of all those you have given me. Amen."

Thursday, March 8, 2018

Know that God is
present and ready to converse.

"Jesus, I live in a world of spirits. Protect me from evil in every form. Let me be with you."

Read the gospel: Luke 11:14–23.

Now Jesus was casting out a demon that was mute; when the demon had gone out, the one who had been mute spoke, and the crowds were amazed. But some of them said, "He casts out demons by Beelzebul, the ruler of the demons." Others, to test him, kept demanding from him a sign from heaven. But he knew what they were thinking and said to them, "Every kingdom divided against itself becomes a desert, and house falls on house. If Satan also is divided against himself, how will his kingdom stand?—for you say that I cast out the demons by Beelzebul. Now if I cast out the demons by Beelzebul, by whom do your exorcists cast them out? Therefore they will be your judges. But if it is by the finger of God that I cast out the demons, then the kingdom of God has come to you. When a strong man, fully armed, guards his castle, his property is safe. But when one stronger than he attacks him and overpowers him, he takes away his armor in which he trusted and divides his plunder. Whoever is not with me is against me, and whoever does not gather with me scatters."

Notice what you think and feel as you read the gospel.

Jesus faces constant criticism for the good he does and is even accused of being in league with Satan. Jesus refutes these accusations, and he declares that he has vanquished evil, even Beelzebul, ruler of the demons.

Pray as you are led for yourself and others.

"Lord, I come to you now to seek your protection for me and for all those you have given me. Let evil hold no sway in our lives . . ." (Continue in your own words.)

Listen to Jesus.

Cling to me, child, and you are safe. Do not fear the arrow that flies by night, but reach out for the light that is the love of God. Let it fill your heart and you will be safe and become a safe harbor yourself for those I have given you. Do you believe me? What else is Jesus saying to you?

Ask God to show you how to live today.

"Lord, I do believe you, but you know my powers are limited. But in you, with you, I can do anything. Let me do some good today, Blessed Savior. Amen."

Friday, March 9, 2018

**Know that God is
present and ready to converse.**

"Lord, you draw near to me now. I will receive the wisdom of your Word."

Read the gospel: Mark 12:28–34.

One of the scribes came near and heard them disputing with one another, and seeing that Jesus answered them well, he asked him, "Which commandment is the first of all?" Jesus answered, "The first is, 'Hear, O Israel: the Lord our God, the Lord is one; you shall love the Lord your God with all your heart, and with all your soul, and with all your mind, and with all your strength.' The second is this, 'You shall love your neighbor as yourself.' There is no other commandment greater than these." Then the scribe said to him, "You are right, Teacher; you have truly said that 'he is one, and besides him there is no other'; and 'to love him with all the heart, and with all the understanding, and with all the strength,' and 'to love one's neighbor as oneself,'—this is much more important than all whole burnt offerings and sacrifices." When Jesus saw that he answered wisely, he said to him, "You are not far from the kingdom of God." After that no one dared to ask him any question.

**Notice what you think
and feel as you read the gospel.**

Jesus and the scribe agree that the commandments to love God with all your being and to love your neighbor as yourself far surpass all other laws, sacrifices, and rituals.

Pray as you are led for yourself and others.

"Lord, give me the grace to love God and others with all my might. In love, I present to you now those you have given me . . ." (Continue in your own words.)

Listen to Jesus.

It's easy to love God if you know God and how much God loves you. All things work together for good for you, my beloved, because you love God. What else is Jesus saying to you?

Ask God to show you how to live today.

"Let the love of God overflow to others today, Lord. And show me what it means to love my neighbor as myself. Amen."

Saturday, March 10, 2018

Know that God is present and ready to converse.

"Lord, you take the initiative, drawing me to prayer and to your Word. I will receive it with joy."

Read the gospel: Luke 18:9–14.

Jesus also told this parable to some who trusted in themselves that they were righteous and regarded others with contempt: "Two men went up to the temple to pray, one a Pharisee and the other a tax collector. The Pharisee, standing by himself, was praying thus, 'God, I thank you that I am not like other people: thieves, rogues, adulterers, or even like this tax collector. I fast twice a week; I give a tenth of all my income.' But the tax collector, standing far off, would not even look up to heaven, but was beating his breast and saying, 'God, be merciful to me, a sinner!' I tell you, this man went down to his home justified rather than the other; for all who exalt themselves will be humbled, but all who humble themselves will be exalted."

Notice what you think and feel as you read the gospel.

It is human nature to regard yourself as the Pharisee does, comparing yourself favorably to sinners and cataloging your virtues. Jesus says those who exalt themselves will be humbled. But those who humble themselves, like the tax collector beating his breast and begging for mercy, will be exalted.

Pray as you are led for yourself and others.

"Lord, your spiritual laws prevail still. To go down is to go up. Be merciful to me, a sinner. Be merciful to those who pride themselves on their virtues, for they are sinners too . . ." (Continue in your own words.)

Listen to Jesus.

Learn from me, for I am perfect, yet I extend mercy to all. Show mercy and do not judge, for the standard by which you judge will be held against you. What else is Jesus saying to you?

Ask God to show you how to live today.

"Lord, it is easy to make fleeting, unpremeditated judgments of others during my day. Arrest them in me before I make them. If I do make a judgment, let me unmake it with mercy. Amen."

FOURTH WEEK OF LENT

A holy longing for God wells up in the heart of believers because they know that the Gospel is not an event of the past but of the present. A holy longing for God helps us keep alert in the face of every attempt to reduce and impoverish our life. A holy longing for God is the memory of faith, which rebels before all prophets of doom. That longing keeps hope alive in the community of believers, which from week to week continues to plead: "Come, Lord Jesus."

Pope Francis
January 6, 2017

Sunday, March 11, 2018
Fourth Sunday of Lent

Know that God is
present and ready to converse.

"Glory to you, Father, Son, and Holy Spirit. I enter your presence with a heart open to your Word."

Read the gospel: John 3:14–21.

Jesus said, "And just as Moses lifted up the serpent in the wilderness, so must the Son of Man be lifted up, that whoever believes in him may have eternal life.

"For God so loved the world that he gave his only Son, so that everyone who believes in him may not perish but may have eternal life.

"Indeed, God did not send the Son into the world to condemn the world, but in order that the world might be saved through him. Those who believe in him are not condemned; but those who do not believe are condemned already, because they have not believed in the name of the only Son of God. And this is the judgment, that the light has come into the world, and people loved darkness rather than light because their deeds were evil. For all who do evil hate the light and do not come to the light, so that their deeds may not be exposed. But those who do what is true come to the light, so that it may be clearly seen that their deeds have been done in God."

Notice what you think
and feel as you read the gospel.

Jesus speaks of his crucifixion and says that he will save all those who look to him. He is the Savior of the world, bringing mercy, light, and eternal life to all who come to him.

Pray as you are led for yourself and others.

"Lord, let me not be blind to my sins. Reveal to me the sins I hide from myself and let me be cleansed by repenting in your grace . . ." (Continue in your own words.)

Listen to Jesus.

I will do it, dear child. I am shedding my light upon you. Do you see it? What else is Jesus saying to you?

Ask God to show you how to live today.

"As I walk in your light today, Lord, let me see others with clarity and compassion, for they are your children. Thank you. Amen."

Monday, March 12, 2018

Know that God is
present and ready to converse.

"Lord, I am with you. Let me receive your Word with faith."

Read the gospel: John 4:43–54.

When the two days were over, Jesus went from that place to Galilee (for Jesus himself had testified that a prophet has no honor in the prophet's own country). When he came to Galilee, the Galileans welcomed him, since they had seen all that he had done in Jerusalem at the festival; for they too had gone to the festival.

Then he came again to Cana in Galilee where he had changed the water into wine. Now there was a royal official whose son lay ill in Capernaum. When he heard that Jesus had come from Judea to Galilee, he went and begged him to come down and heal his son, for he was at the point of death. Then Jesus said to him, "Unless you see signs and wonders you will not believe." The official said to him, "Sir, come down before my little boy dies." Jesus said to him,

"Go; your son will live." The man believed the word that Jesus spoke to him and started on his way. As he was going down, his slaves met him and told him that his child was alive. So he asked them the hour when he began to recover, and they said to him, "Yesterday at one in the afternoon the fever left him." The father realized that this was the hour when Jesus had said to him, "Your son will live." So he himself believed, along with his whole household. Now this was the second sign that Jesus did after coming from Judea to Galilee.

Notice what you think and feel as you read the gospel.

Jesus apparently challenges the man, who seems as if he wants only a sign. But the man is worried that his sick son might die. Jesus pronounces the son healed, and the man believes; his son is healed when he arrives home, and his whole household believes in Jesus.

Pray as you are led for yourself and others.

"Lord, increase my faith. Help my unbelief. Let me believe what is true about God. I pray, too, that others will find true faith . . ." (Continue in your own words.)

Listen to Jesus.

I am pleased by faith, beloved. Faith may be small but it endures and it grows. It makes all the difference to me and to you. Believe me. What else is Jesus saying to you?

Ask God to show you how to live today.

"I am a person of little faith; I am afraid. Let me do something in faith today, Lord. Teach me to live in faith. Amen."

Tuesday, March 13, 2018

Know that God is
present and ready to converse.

"God, you are with me before I can come to you. You
see me as I am, full of needs only you can satisfy. Let
me feed on your holy Word."

Read the gospel: John 5:1–16.

After this there was a festival of the Jews, and Jesus
went up to Jerusalem.

   Now in Jerusalem by the Sheep Gate there is a pool,
called in Hebrew Beth-zatha, which has five porticoes.
In these lay many invalids—blind, lame, and para-
lyzed. One man was there who had been ill for thir-
ty-eight years. When Jesus saw him lying there and
knew that he had been there a long time, he said to
him, "Do you want to be made well?" The sick man
answered him, "Sir, I have no one to put me into the
pool when the water is stirred up; and while I am making my way, someone else steps down ahead of me."
Jesus said to him, "Stand up, take your mat and walk."
At once the man was made well, and he took up his
mat and began to walk.

   Now that day was a sabbath. So the Jews said to the
man who had been cured, "It is the sabbath; it is not
lawful for you to carry your mat." But he answered
them, "The man who made me well said to me, 'Take
up your mat and walk.'" They asked him, "Who is the
man who said to you, 'Take it up and walk'?" Now the

man who had been healed did not know who it was, for Jesus had disappeared in the crowd that was there. Later Jesus found him in the temple and said to him, "See, you have been made well! Do not sin any more, so that nothing worse happens to you." The man went away and told the Jews that it was Jesus who had made him well. Therefore the Jews started persecuting Jesus, because he was doing such things on the sabbath.

Notice what you think and feel as you read the gospel.

Jesus takes the initiative to heal the invalid by the miraculous pool, Beth-zatha. The local Jews find fault in this because he has healed on the Sabbath, and they begin to persecute him.

Pray as you are led for yourself and others.

"Lord, you know where I am sick and sinful. Heal me, forgive me, and let me glorify God . . ." (Continue in your own words.)

Listen to Jesus.

My beloved, I am with you. Offer yourself to God today for the good of others. In that you will find healing and forgiveness. What else is Jesus saying to you?

Ask God to show you how to live today.

"Lord, you have made me well. I am yours, your servant. Do with me what you will. Amen."

Wednesday, March 14, 2018

Know that God is
present and ready to converse.

"Three-Person God, you are One. Let me be one with
you by the healing power of your Word."

Read the gospel: John 5:17–30.

But Jesus answered them, "My Father is still working,
and I also am working." For this reason the Jews were
seeking all the more to kill him, because he was not
only breaking the sabbath, but was also calling God
his own Father, thereby making himself equal to God.

Jesus said to them, "Very truly, I tell you, the Son
can do nothing on his own, but only what he sees the
Father doing; for whatever the Father does, the Son
does likewise. The Father loves the Son and shows
him all that he himself is doing; and he will show him
greater works than these, so that you will be astonished. Indeed, just as the Father raises the dead and
gives them life, so also the Son gives life to whom-
soever he wishes. The Father judges no one but has
given all judgement to the Son, so that all may honor
the Son just as they honor the Father. Anyone who does
not honor the Son does not honor the Father who sent
him. Very truly, I tell you, anyone who hears my word
and believes him who sent me has eternal life, and
does not come under judgement, but has passed from
death to life.

"Very truly, I tell you, the hour is coming, and is now here, when the dead will hear the voice of the Son of God, and those who hear will live. For just as the Father has life in himself, so he has granted the Son also to have life in himself; and he has given him authority to execute judgement, because he is the Son of Man. Do not be astonished at this; for the hour is coming when all who are in their graves will hear his voice and will come out—those who have done good, to the resurrection of life, and those who have done evil, to the resurrection of condemnation.

"I can do nothing on my own. As I hear, I judge; and my judgement is just, because I seek to do not my own will but the will of him who sent me."

Notice what you think and feel as you read the gospel.

Jesus does the will and the work of his Father. To receive Jesus as the Son of God is to honor the Father who sent him. To receive him is to receive eternal life. Those who hear and believe have already passed from death to life. The judgment is coming, with resurrection to condemnation or to life.

Pray as you are led for yourself and others.

"Jesus, I believe you are the Son of God, one with God. Thank you for coming and doing your merciful works among us. I pray for those who resist you, that they may truly hear and believe . . ." (Continue in your own words.)

Listen to Jesus.

I hear your prayers, beloved. Your will and my will are the same. I will work as you ask. Trust me. What else is Jesus saying to you?

Ask God to show you how to live today.

"I seek to do not my will today, but yours. If there are things I can do or say or pray, prompt me, Lord, and I will obey. Amen."

Thursday, March 15, 2018

Know that God is present and ready to converse.

"Lord, your being here with me speaks of the reality of God—Father, Son, and Holy Spirit. Speak to me also through your Word."

Read the gospel: John 5:31–47.

Jesus said, "If I testify about myself, my testimony is not true. There is another who testifies on my behalf, and I know that his testimony to me is true. You sent messengers to John, and he testified to the truth. Not that I accept such human testimony, but I say these things so that you may be saved. He was a burning and shining lamp, and you were willing to rejoice for a while in his light. But I have a testimony greater than John's. The works that the Father has given me to complete, the very works that I am doing, testify on my behalf that the Father has sent me. And the Father who sent me has himself testified on my behalf. You have never heard his voice or seen his form, and you do not have his word abiding in you, because you do not believe him whom he has sent.

"You search the scriptures because you think that in them you have eternal life; and it is they that testify on my behalf. Yet you refuse to come to me to have life. I do not accept glory from human beings. But I know that you do not have the love of God in you. I have come in my Father's name, and you do not accept me; if another comes in his own name, you will accept him. How can you believe when you accept glory from one another and do not seek the glory that comes from the one who alone is God? Do not think that I will accuse you before the Father; your accuser is Moses, on whom you have set your hope. If you believed Moses, you would believe me, for he wrote about me. But if you do not believe what he wrote, how will you believe what I say?"

Notice what you think and feel as you read the gospel.

Jesus has testimony from John, from his Father, from the works he does, and from scripture, including Moses—yet his hearers will not believe in him. They are stuck in their human ways of thinking.

Pray as you are led for yourself and others.

"What will make the unbelieving world give true consideration to you, Jesus? This is the time of gathering—gather them in, Lord . . ." (Continue in your own words.)

Listen to Jesus.

Yes, gathering is the purpose of this age, which is rapidly moving toward its end. Your faith in me has a great influence on those I have given you. Simply stay close to me, beloved. What else is Jesus saying to you?

Ask God to show you how to live today.

"I come to you to have life, Jesus; stay close to me. Amen."

Friday, March 16, 2018

Know that God is
present and ready to converse.

"Increase my faith in you, Lord, for faith is a gift of God. Let your Word increase my faith."

Read the gospel: John 7:1–2, 10, 25–30.

After this Jesus went about in Galilee. He did not wish to go about in Judea because the Jews were looking for an opportunity to kill him. Now the Jewish festival of Booths was near. . . .

But after his brothers had gone to the festival, then he also went, not publicly but as it were in secret. . . .

Now some of the people of Jerusalem were saying, "Is not this the man whom they are trying to kill? And here he is, speaking openly, but they say nothing to him! Can it be that the authorities really know that this is the Messiah? Yet we know where this man is from; but when the Messiah comes, no one will know where he is from." Then Jesus cried out as he was teaching in the temple, "You know me, and you know where I am from. I have not come on my own. But the one who sent me is true, and you do not know him. I know him, because I am from him, and he sent me." Then they tried to arrest him, but no one laid hands on him, because his hour had not yet come.

Notice what you think and feel as you read the gospel.

In Judea, they are seeking an opportunity to kill Jesus, yet still he goes down to Jerusalem and speaks openly in the temple. Some of the people remark that he cannot be the Messiah because they know where he comes from and no one will know where the Messiah is from. Jesus admits that they know where he is from yet says that they do not know who sent him, the true God. But no one lays hands on him because his time has not yet come.

Pray as you are led for yourself and others.

"Jesus, so much of your life you faced rejection and contradiction, arguments, jealousy, and rage. Soon they will arrest you and crucify you. Lord, strengthen me against rejection. I offer it all to you on behalf of those I pray for now . . ." (Continue in your own words.)

Listen to Jesus.

Do not be afraid, dear friend. I am with you, especially in your sufferings. Let your suffering be one with mine for the redemption of others. What else is Jesus saying to you?

Ask God to show you how to live today.

"Remind me to lift my suffering to you today, and let it bear fruit to your glory. Amen."

Saturday, March 17, 2018

Know that God is present and ready to converse.

"Lord, dispel my darkness by your Word. Be my light."

Read the gospel: John 7:40–53.

When they heard Jesus' words, some in the crowd said, "This is really the prophet." Others said, "This is the Messiah." But some asked, "Surely the Messiah does not come from Galilee, does he? Has not the scripture said that the Messiah is descended from David and comes from Bethlehem, the village where David lived?" So there was a division in the crowd because of him. Some of them wanted to arrest him, but no one laid hands on him.

Then the temple police went back to the chief priests and Pharisees, who asked them, "Why did you not arrest him?" The police answered, "Never has anyone spoken like this!" Then the Pharisees replied, "Surely you have not been deceived too, have you? Has any one of the authorities or of the Pharisees believed in him? But this crowd, which does not know the law—they are accursed." Nicodemus, who had gone to Jesus before, and who was one of them, asked, "Our law does not judge people without first giving them a hearing to find out what they are doing, does it?" They replied, "Surely you are not also from Galilee, are you? Search and you will see that no prophet is to arise from Galilee." Then each of them went home.

Notice what you think and feel as you read the gospel.

The people argue among themselves with considerable ignorance, for Jesus is descended from David and from Bethlehem. Though commissioned to arrest Jesus by the chief priests, the temple police fail to do so, for they are amazed at Jesus: "Never has anyone spoken like this!" Nicodemus urges the people to hear and consider what Jesus says and does before they make judgments.

Pray as you are led for yourself and others.

"Lord, keep me open to you and your Word, that I may know and love the truth. I pray that all those you have given me may come to know and love your truth, for you, Jesus, are the Truth . . ." (Continue in your own words.)

Listen to Jesus.

People generally do what they want to do, and they shape their own thinking around their desires. I am asking you to do what I want and desire, for that will make you truly happy and it will do much good for others. What else is Jesus saying to you?

Ask God to show you how to live today.

"I wish I could just give you all my will in one moment, but I need to offer myself to you day by day, moment by moment. Take me, Lord. Amen."

FIFTH WEEK OF LENT

Communication has the power to build bridges, to enable encounter and inclusion, and thus to enrich society. How beautiful it is when people select their words and actions with care, in the effort to avoid misunderstandings, to heal wounded memories and to build peace and harmony. Words can build bridges between individuals and within families, social groups and peoples. This is possible both in the material world and the digital world. Our words and actions should be such as to help us all escape the vicious circles of condemnation and vengeance which continue to ensnare individuals and nations, encouraging expressions of hatred. The words of Christians ought to be a constant encouragement to communion and, even in those cases where they must firmly condemn evil, they should never try to rupture relationships and communication.

Pope Francis
January 24, 2016

Sunday, March 18, 2018
Fifth Sunday of Lent

Know that God is
present and ready to converse.

"Speak the Word, O Lord, and I will come forth into your Resurrection and your Life."

Read the gospel: John 12:20–33.

Now among those who went up to worship at the festival were some Greeks. They came to Philip, who was from Bethsaida in Galilee, and said to him, "Sir, we wish to see Jesus." Philip went and told Andrew; then Andrew and Philip went and told Jesus. Jesus answered them, "The hour has come for the Son of Man to be glorified. Very truly, I tell you, unless a grain of wheat falls into the earth and dies, it remains just a single grain; but if it dies, it bears much fruit. Those who love their life lose it, and those who hate their life in this world will keep it for eternal life. Whoever serves me must follow me, and where I am, there will my servant be also. Whoever serves me, the Father will honor.

"Now my soul is troubled. And what should I say—'Father, save me from this hour'? No, it is for this reason that I have come to this hour. Father, glorify your name." Then a voice came from heaven, "I have glorified it, and I will glorify it again." The crowd standing there heard it and said that it was thunder. Others said, "An angel has spoken to him." Jesus answered, "This voice has come for your sake, not for mine. Now is the judgment of this world; now the ruler of this world will be driven out. And I, when I am lifted up from the earth, will draw all people to myself." He said this to indicate the kind of death he was to die.

Notice what you think and feel as you read the gospel.

Jesus teaches his disciples that, paradoxically, death is the way to life. They must be willing to lose their lives, as he will, to inherit eternal life.

Pray as you are led for yourself and others.

"Lord, I am willing to lose my life to gain my life. I pray for myself and all those who are afraid . . ." (Continue in your own words.)

Listen to Jesus.

My child, you too face death, with me or without me. Cling to me, follow me, and I will bring you through. I will bless those you pray for too, for the love you have for them is love I give you. What else is Jesus saying to you?

Ask God to show you how to live today.

"Help me cling to you, Lord, not to my life. Where you go, I will follow, for I am your servant. Help me to cast down my life today in service of others; let me be available to others today, my Jesus, and give me ways to care and to help. Amen."

Monday, March 19, 2018
Saint Joseph, Husband of Mary

Know that God is
present and ready to converse.

"Lord, you guide me by your Word and your Spirit. I rejoice in your presence."

Read the gospel: Matthew 1:16, 18–21, 24a.

And Jacob [was] the father of Joseph the husband of Mary, of whom Jesus was born, who is called the Messiah. . . .

Now the birth of Jesus the Messiah took place in this way. When his mother Mary had been engaged to Joseph, but before they lived together, she was found to be with child from the Holy Spirit. Her husband Joseph, being a righteous man and unwilling to expose her to public disgrace, planned to dismiss her quietly. But just when he had resolved to do this, an angel of the Lord appeared to him in a dream and said, "Joseph, son of David, do not be afraid to take Mary as your wife, for the child conceived in her is from the Holy Spirit. She will bear a son, and you are to name him Jesus, for he will save his people from their sins.". . .

When Joseph awoke from sleep, he did as the angel of the Lord commanded him; he took her as his wife.

Notice what you think and feel as you read the gospel.

Joseph, a righteous man, wishes to protect the pregnant Mary from public disgrace by dismissing her quietly. But the angel in his dream tells him to go ahead and marry her, for the child is from the Holy Spirit. Joseph believes and obeys. It must have felt to Joseph like an undeniable word from God.

Pray as you are led for yourself and others.

"Sometimes a spiritual moment can have an unusual power of reality, more real than ordinary moments. Speak to your people, Lord, and let them know you and receive your guidance . . ." (Continue in your own words.)

Listen to Jesus.

I speak to you, beloved disciple. Let those who wish to hear, hear my voice. I am ready to guide each one in the way of life everlasting. What else is Jesus saying to you?

Ask God to show you how to live today.

"Lord, speak to me today, and open my heart that I may follow not my own ideas of righteousness but your perfect will. Amen."

Tuesday, March 20, 2018

Know that God is present and ready to converse.

"Jesus, wholly God and wholly man, you are mystery. Let me learn of you through your Word."

Read the gospel: John 8:21–30.

Again Jesus said to the Pharisees, "I am going away, and you will search for me, but you will die in your sin. Where I am going, you cannot come." Then the Jews said, "Is he going to kill himself? Is that what he means by saying, 'Where I am going, you cannot come'?" He said to them, "You are from below, I am from above; you are of this world, I am not of this world. I told you that you would die in your sins, for you will die in your sins unless you believe that I am he." They said to him, "Who are you?" Jesus said to them, "Why do I speak to you at all? I have much to say about you and much to condemn; but the one who sent me is true, and I declare to the world what I have heard from him." They did not understand that he was speaking to them about the Father. So Jesus said, "When you have lifted up the Son of Man, then you will realize that I am he, and that I do nothing on my own, but I speak these things as the Father instructed me. And the one who sent me is with me; he has not left me alone, for I always do what is pleasing to him." As he was saying these things, many believed in him.

Notice what you think and feel as you read the gospel.

The Jews do not understand what Jesus is telling them—about himself, about them. They are of this world, below; he is from the Father, above. He warns them that they will die in their sins unless they believe that he is the Messiah. He foretells his death and says it will be a clear sign to them who he is and who sent him. Many believed in him.

Pray as you are led for yourself and others.

"How wonderful that the Crucifixion is the proof of the Messiah! It shows that you are from the Father and bring love for all humanity. I pray that others may come to know this love . . ." (Continue in your own words.)

Listen to Jesus.

I gave myself for you. I give myself to you now. We are one with all who are in God. Eternal life has already begun in you, beloved. What else is Jesus saying to you?

Ask God to show you how to live today.

"Let this be a day to anticipate with love your Passion and Death. Make it real to me, so that it changes my life and brings me closer to you. Amen."

Wednesday, March 21, 2018

Know that God is
present and ready to converse.

"Lord, I return to your Word, and I find you waiting here for me. Thank you."

Read the gospel: John 8:31–42.

Then Jesus said to the Jews who had believed in him, "If you continue in my word, you are truly my disciples; and you will know the truth, and the truth will make you free." They answered him, "We are descendants of Abraham and have never been slaves to anyone. What do you mean by saying, 'You will be made free'?"

Jesus answered them, "Very truly, I tell you, everyone who commits sin is a slave to sin. The slave does not have a permanent place in the household; the son has a place there forever. So if the Son makes you free, you will be free indeed. I know that you are descendants of Abraham; yet you look for an opportunity to kill me, because there is no place in you for my word. I declare what I have seen in the Father's presence; as for you, you should do what you have heard from the Father."

They answered him, "Abraham is our father." Jesus said to them, "If you were Abraham's children, you would be doing what Abraham did, but now you are trying to kill me, a man who has told you the truth that I heard from God. This is not what Abraham did. You are indeed doing what your father does." They said to him, "We are not illegitimate children; we have one father, God himself." Jesus said to them, "If God were your Father, you would love me, for I came from God and now I am here. I did not come on my own, but he sent me."

Notice what you think and feel as you read the gospel.

Jesus tells his listeners that they should do what you have heard from the Father. They claim God as Father, but Jesus says that if this were true, they would love him, for he came from God. He is the truth that makes his disciples free.

Pray as you are led for yourself and others.

"Lord, I love you. Thank you for setting me free. I pray earnestly for those you have given me. Let them love you too and walk in your freedom . . ." (Continue in your own words.)

Listen to Jesus.

Examine your life, beloved, and identify what enslaves you, what hinders your freedom. Seek my grace to remove those sins from your life. I want you to walk in truth and be free. What else is Jesus saying to you?

Ask God to show you how to live today.

"Let me take your words to heart, Lord. Help me examine my life and break free of the things that enslave me, especially habitual sins. Amen."

Thursday, March 22, 2018

**Know that God is
present and ready to converse.**

"Jesus, Teacher, speak to me plainly through your holy Word. Holy Spirit, guide me."

Read the gospel: John 8:51–59.

Jesus said, "Very truly, I tell you, whoever keeps my word will never see death." The Jews said to him, "Now we know that you have a demon. Abraham died, and so did the prophets; yet you say, 'Whoever keeps my word will never taste death.' Are you greater than our father Abraham, who died? The prophets also died. Who do you claim to be?" Jesus answered, "If I glorify myself, my glory is nothing. It is my Father who glorifies me, he of whom you say, 'He is our God,' though you do not know him. But I know him; if I were to say that I do not know him, I would be a liar like you. But I do know him and I keep his word. Your ancestor Abraham rejoiced that he would see my day; he saw it and was glad." Then the Jews said to him, "You are not yet fifty years old, and have you seen Abraham?" Jesus said to them, "Very truly, I tell you, before Abraham was, I am." So they picked up stones to throw at him, but Jesus hid himself and went out of the temple.

Notice what you think and feel as you read the gospel.

The Jews continue to argue with Jesus. They cannot believe Jesus is the Son of God, one with the Father. When he tells them plainly who he is, they attempt to stone him for blasphemy.

Pray as you are led for yourself and others.

"Lord, I believe in you. Help me keep your word and never see death. I pray others also find saving faith in you . . ." (Continue in your own words.)

Listen to Jesus.

I ask my disciples to keep my commandments and to proclaim the Gospel to the whole world. I will help you do your part, dear friend. What else is Jesus saying to you?

Ask God to show you how to live today.

"Let me receive your help to keep your word and thus to do and say what you want. Thank you for being with me, Jesus. Amen."

Friday, March 23, 2018

Know that God is
present and ready to converse.

"Son of God, you are good to me. I praise you for your glory."

Read the gospel: John 10:31–42.

The Jews took up stones again to stone him. Jesus replied, "I have shown you many good works from the Father. For which of these are you going to stone me?" The Jews answered, "It is not for a good work that we are going to stone you, but for blasphemy, because you, though only a human being, are making yourself God." Jesus answered, "Is it not written in your law, 'I said, you are gods'? If those to whom the word of God came were called 'gods'—and the scripture cannot be annulled—can you say that the one whom the Father has sanctified and sent into the world is blaspheming because I said, 'I am God's Son'? If I am not doing the works of my Father, then do not believe me. But if I do them, even though you do not believe me, believe the works, so that you may know and understand that the Father is in me and I am in the Father." Then they tried to arrest him again, but he escaped from their hands.

He went away again across the Jordan to the place where John had been baptizing earlier, and he remained there. Many came to him, and they were saying, "John performed no sign, but everything that John said about this man was true." And many believed in him there.

Notice what you think and feel as you read the gospel.

Jesus answers his adversaries well, and he backs up his words with healings and mighty miracles. He says the Father sent him into the world to tell us that he is God's Son, and he does the good works of God, yet they call him a blasphemer and want to arrest him.

Pray as you are led for yourself and others.

"Lord, many oppose you and deny your divinity, often bitterly. I pray for them, and I thank you for being willing to suffer such rejection. I don't reject you, Jesus. I am yours . . ." (Continue in your own words.)

Listen to Jesus.

Your words show understanding and your heart consoles me. You are the reason I was willing to suffer and die. Those who follow me continue to suffer and die. They are precious to me. What else is Jesus saying to you?

Ask God to show you how to live today.

"Lord, let me walk your Way of the Cross today, in solidarity with all those who suffer for your name. Amen."

Saturday, March 24, 2018

Know that God is present and ready to converse.

"Jesus, I am often concerned with earthly things. Let me turn from them and contemplate heavenly things in your Word."

Read the gospel: John 11:45–56.

Many of the Jews therefore, who had come with Mary and had seen what Jesus did, believed in him. But some of them went to the Pharisees and told them what he had done. So the chief priests and the Pharisees called a meeting of the council, and said, "What are we to do? This man is performing many signs. If we let him go on like this, everyone will believe in him, and the Romans will come and destroy both our holy place and our nation." But one of them, Caiaphas, who was high priest that year, said to them, "You know nothing at all! You do not understand that it is better for you to have one man die for the people than to have the whole nation destroyed." He did not say this on his own, but being high priest that year he prophesied that Jesus was about to die for the nation, and not for the nation only, but to gather into one the dispersed children of God. So from that day on they planned to put him to death.

Jesus therefore no longer walked about openly among the Jews, but went from there to a town called

Ephraim in the region near the wilderness; and he remained there with the disciples.

Now the Passover of the Jews was near, and many went up from the country to Jerusalem before the Passover to purify themselves. They were looking for Jesus and were asking one another as they stood in the temple, "What do you think? Surely he will not come to the festival, will he?"

Notice what you think and feel as you read the gospel.

After Jesus raises Lazarus from the dead, some Jews report it to the council of priests. They are worried that so many are coming to believe in Jesus that the Romans will come and destroy their temple and their nation. Caiaphas, the high priest, says that one man could die as a scapegoat for the nation, unwittingly prophesying that Jesus was about to die not only for the nation but to gather into one all the children of God everywhere. The council plans to put Jesus to death.

Pray as you are led for yourself and others.

"What folly in human plans, Lord, even my own. I turn my life over to you to manage. Let me serve you and these others I pray for . . ." (Continue in your own words.)

Listen to Jesus.

Have no fear, beloved child, for I am with you. Rejoice in the providence of God. I will bless you as you follow me. What else is Jesus saying to you?

Ask God to show you how to live today.

"I resolve today to follow you, accepting the circumstances you give me, and trusting in God's providence to bring good even out of evil. Amen."

HOLY WEEK

May we realize that we are all begging for God's love, and not allow ourselves to miss the Lord as he passes by.

Pope Francis
March 4, 2016

Sunday, March 25, 2018
Palm Sunday of the Lord's Passion

Know that God is
present and ready to converse.

"Jesus, the gospels are your story. Let me know you
through your Word."

Read the gospel: Mark
14:1–15 (Mk 14:1–15:47).

It was two days before the Passover and the festival
of Unleavened Bread. The chief priests and the scribes
were looking for a way to arrest Jesus by stealth and
kill him; for they said, "Not during the festival, or there
may be a riot among the people."

While he was at Bethany in the house of Simon the
leper, as he sat at the table, a woman came with an
alabaster jar of very costly ointment of nard, and she
broke open the jar and poured the ointment on his
head. But some were there who said to one another in
anger, "Why was the ointment wasted in this way? For
this ointment could have been sold for more than three
hundred denarii, and the money given to the poor."
And they scolded her. But Jesus said, "Let her alone;
why do you trouble her? She has performed a good
service for me. For you always have the poor with you,
and you can show kindness to them whenever you
wish; but you will not always have me. She has done
what she could; she has anointed my body beforehand
for its burial. Truly I tell you, wherever the good news

is proclaimed in the whole world, what she has done will be told in remembrance of her."

Then Judas Iscariot, who was one of the twelve, went to the chief priests in order to betray him to them. When they heard it, they were greatly pleased, and promised to give him money. So he began to look for an opportunity to betray him.

On the first day of Unleavened Bread, when the Passover lamb is sacrificed, his disciples said to him, "Where do you want us to go and make the preparations for you to eat the Passover?" So he sent two of his disciples, saying to them, "Go into the city, and a man carrying a jar of water will meet you; follow him, and wherever he enters, say to the owner of the house, 'The Teacher asks, Where is my guest room where I may eat the Passover with my disciples?' He will show you a large room upstairs, furnished and ready. Make preparations for us there."

Notice what you think and feel as you read the gospel.

The chief priests and Pharisees are looking for a way to capture Jesus by stealth and kill him. A woman honors Jesus by pouring a costly ointment on his head. When some object to the waste of money, Jesus commends the woman for anointing his body for burial because he knows his time of death is near. Judas goes to the chief priests to betray him. Two of his disciples are directed by Jesus to find a room for their Passover meal.

Pray as you are led for yourself and others.

"Jesus, you know all and can do all things. Show me what I need to know and do. Let me be your hands and feet, serving and praying for those you have given me . . ." (Continue in your own words.)

Listen to Jesus.

Her extravagant love — that's what I appreciated about the woman who anointed my head in the house of Simon. True love doesn't count the cost but expresses itself in ways large and small. What else is Jesus saying to you?

Ask God to show you how to live today.

"Help me to love like that, Lord, for I want to please you. Thank you. Amen."

Monday, March 26, 2018

**Know that God is
present and ready to converse.**

"Holy Spirit, be with me and help me discern the Word of Truth before me."

Read the gospel: John 12:1–11.

Six days before the Passover Jesus came to Bethany, the home of Lazarus, whom he had raised from the dead. There they gave a dinner for him. Martha served, and Lazarus was one of those at the table with him. Mary took a pound of costly perfume made of pure nard, anointed Jesus' feet, and wiped them with her hair. The house was filled with the fragrance of the perfume. But Judas Iscariot, one of his disciples (the one who was about to betray him), said, "Why was this perfume not sold for three hundred denarii and the money given to the poor?" (He said this not because he cared about the poor, but because he was a thief; he kept the common purse and used to steal what was put into it.) Jesus said, "Leave her alone. She bought it so that she might keep it for the day of my burial. You always have the poor with you, but you do not always have me."

When the great crowd of the Jews learned that he was there, they came not only because of Jesus but also to see Lazarus, whom he had raised from the dead. So the chief priests planned to put Lazarus to death as well, since it was on account of him that many of the Jews were deserting and were believing in Jesus.

Notice what you think and feel as you read the gospel.

Mary of Bethany anoints Jesus' feet with perfume. Judas complains the perfume should have been sold and the money given to the poor, though his real purpose was to have more money to steal from the common purse. Many were at the house to see both Jesus and Lazarus, whom Jesus had raised from the dead. The priests planned to put Lazarus to death as well. How threatened they must have felt by the growth of Jesus' following.

Pray as you are led for yourself and others.

"Lord, you must have felt fear as your time of Passion and Death neared. You were human too, divine Savior. I pray for all those who live in fear. Give them peace, Lord . . ." (Continue in your own words.)

Listen to Jesus.

Yes, I knew fear, but knowing my Father of perfect light and love allowed me to master the fear. I tell you that secret, beloved disciple. What else is Jesus saying to you?

Ask God to show you how to live today.

"Let me face my own fears as you did, Jesus. Let me trust in the Father's infinite love and kindness and the perfect wisdom of his providence in my life. Amen."

Tuesday, March 27, 2018

**Know that God is
present and ready to converse.**

"Jesus, I am trying to follow you, to know and love you better, by reading your Word. Thank you for being here with me and guiding me."

Read the gospel: John 13:21–33, 36–38.

After saying this Jesus was troubled in spirit, and declared, "Very truly, I tell you, one of you will betray me." The disciples looked at one another, uncertain of whom he was speaking. One of his disciples—the one whom Jesus loved—was reclining next to him; Simon Peter therefore motioned to him to ask Jesus of whom he was speaking. So while reclining next to Jesus, he asked him, "Lord, who is it?" Jesus answered, "It is the one to whom I give this piece of bread when I have dipped it in the dish." So when he had dipped the piece of bread, he gave it to Judas son of Simon Iscariot. After he received the piece of bread, Satan entered into him. Jesus said to him, "Do quickly what you are going to do." Now no one at the table knew why he said this to him. Some thought that, because Judas had the common purse, Jesus was telling him, "Buy what we need for the festival"; or, that he should give something to the poor. So, after receiving the piece of bread, he immediately went out. And it was night.

When he had gone out, Jesus said, "Now the Son of Man has been glorified, and God has been glorified in him. If God has been glorified in him, God will also glorify him in himself and will glorify him at once. Little children, I am with you only a little longer. You will look for me; and as I said to the Jews so now I say to you, 'Where I am going, you cannot come.'" . . .

Simon Peter said to him, "Lord, where are you going?" Jesus answered, "Where I am going, you cannot follow me now; but you will follow afterwards." Peter said to him, "Lord, why can I not follow you now? I will lay down my life for you." Jesus answered, "Will you lay down your life for me? Very truly, I tell you, before the cock crows, you will have denied me three times."

Notice what you think and feel as you read the gospel.

Jesus is troubled by Judas's betrayal, but he knows it is necessary. Jesus sees his Passion and Death as his glorification, part and parcel of his Resurrection and Ascension. He prepares his disciples for his departure and predicts Peter's denial of him.

Pray as you are led for yourself and others.

"Lord, keep me from thinking that I have achieved full commitment to you. I am just a person, full of weakness and ignorance. Give me strength, wisdom, faith, and love so that I may follow you . . ." (Continue in your own words.)

Listen to Jesus.

You are secure in me. If you stumble and fall, turn to me, and I will pick you up and love you. For you, too, are a little child to me, and you are my own. Spend time with me today. What else is Jesus saying to you?

Ask God to show you how to live today.

"Your love is my strength, Lord. Let me not dwell on my own failures today but receive your forgiveness and love you all the more. Amen."

Wednesday, March 28, 2018

Know that God is
present and ready to converse.

"Lord of heaven and earth, be real to me as I meet you in your Word."

Read the gospel: Matthew 26:14–25.

Then one of the twelve, who was called Judas Iscariot, went to the chief priests and said, "What will you give me if I betray him to you?" They paid him thirty pieces of silver. And from that moment he began to look for an opportunity to betray him.

On the first day of Unleavened Bread the disciples came to Jesus, saying, "Where do you want us to make the preparations for you to eat the Passover?" He said, "Go into the city to a certain man, and say to him, 'The Teacher says, My time is near; I will keep the Passover at your house with my disciples.'" So the disciples did as Jesus had directed them, and they prepared the Passover meal.

When it was evening, he took his place with the twelve; and while they were eating, he said, "Truly I tell you, one of you will betray me." And they became greatly distressed and began to say to him one after another, "Surely not I, Lord?" He answered, "The one who has dipped his hand into the bowl with me will betray me. The Son of Man goes as it is written of him, but woe to that one by whom the Son of Man is betrayed! It would have been better for that one not

to have been born." Judas, who betrayed him, said,
"Surely not I, Rabbi?" He replied, "You have said so."

Notice what you think
and feel as you read the gospel.

Judas betrays Jesus for thirty pieces of silver and then
joins the disciples at the Passover feast. There Jesus
talks about the one who will betray him, and they all
worry it might be themselves. "Surely not I, Lord?"
they ask Jesus. Jesus said it would be better for that
man who betrays him never to have been born.

Pray as you are led for yourself and others.

"Lord, surely not I? Put your guard about me. Let me
be constant and faithful in my devotion and service to
you. I pray the same for all those who follow you and
serve you . . ." (Continue in your own words.)

Listen to Jesus.

*Be simple in your faith in me. Love me as a child loves. Do
not overreach in trying to do or be something I have not
asked of you. Be honest. Be yourself. And be mine. I love you
always.* What else is Jesus saying to you?

Ask God to show you how to live today.

"Help me to walk the simple way with you, my Jesus.
Only you I need. Amen."

Thursday, March 29, 2018
Holy Thursday

Know that God is
present and ready to converse.

"Jesus, thank you for coming. What have you to teach me, Lord?"

Read the gospel: John 13:1–15.

Now before the festival of the Passover, Jesus knew that his hour had come to depart from this world and go to the Father. Having loved his own who were in the world, he loved them to the end. The devil had already put it into the heart of Judas son of Simon Iscariot to betray him. And during supper Jesus, knowing that the Father had given all things into his hands, and that he had come from God and was going to God, got up from the table, took off his outer robe, and tied a towel around himself. Then he poured water into a basin and began to wash the disciples' feet and to wipe them with the towel that was tied around him. He came to Simon Peter, who said to him, "Lord, are you going to wash my feet?" Jesus answered, "You do not know now what I am doing, but later you will understand." Peter said to him, "You will never wash my feet." Jesus answered, "Unless I wash you, you have no share with me." Simon Peter said to him, "Lord, not my feet only but also my hands and my head!" Jesus said to him, "One who has bathed does not need to wash, except for the feet, but is entirely clean. And you are clean, though not all of you." For he knew who was to betray him; for this reason he said, "Not all of you are clean."

After he had washed their feet, had put on his robe, and had returned to the table, he said to them, "Do you know what I have done to you? You call me Teacher and Lord—and you are right, for that is what I am. So if I, your Lord and Teacher, have washed your feet, you also ought to wash one another's feet. For I have set you an example, that you also should do as I have done to you."

Notice what you think and feel as you read the gospel.

Jesus teaches by example as he washes the feet of his disciples. He chooses to spend his last hours by serving his friends, modeling humility.

Pray as you are led for yourself and others.

"Lord, I aspire to your humility. Give me a heart to serve others in every way I can. Let me do unto others as unto you . . ." (Continue in your own words.)

Listen to Jesus.

You don't need to pretend anything, dear child. Be what you are and trust me to form you into the person I want you to be. What else is Jesus saying to you?

Ask God to show you how to live today.

"Linger with me, Lord. I don't want you to leave. I don't want you to suffer and die. How can I help you? Amen."

Friday, March 30, 2018
Good Friday

Know that God is
present and ready to converse.

"Let me contemplate your Passion, Lord, that I may love you more."

Read the gospel: John
18:1–19 (Jn 18:1–19:42).

After Jesus had spoken these words, he went out with his disciples across the Kidron valley to a place where there was a garden, which he and his disciples entered. Now Judas, who betrayed him, also knew the place, because Jesus often met there with his disciples. So Judas brought a detachment of soldiers together with police from the chief priests and the Pharisees, and they came there with lanterns and torches and weapons. Then Jesus, knowing all that was to happen to him, came forward and asked them, "Whom are you looking for?" They answered, "Jesus of Nazareth." Jesus replied, "I am he." Judas, who betrayed him, was standing with them. When Jesus said to them, "I am he," they stepped back and fell to the ground. Again he asked them, "Whom are you looking for?" And they said, "Jesus of Nazareth." Jesus answered, "I told you that I am he. So if you are looking for me, let these men go." This was to fulfill the word that he had spoken, "I did not lose a single one of those whom you gave me." Then Simon Peter, who had a sword, drew it, struck the high priest's slave, and cut off his right ear. The slave's name was Malchus. Jesus said to Peter, "Put your sword back into its sheath. Am I not to drink the cup that the Father has given me?"

So the soldiers, their officer, and the Jewish police arrested Jesus and bound him. First they took him to Annas, who was the father-in-law of Caiaphas, the high priest that year. Caiaphas was the one who had advised the Jews that it was better to have one person die for the people.

Simon Peter and another disciple followed Jesus. Since that disciple was known to the high priest, he went with Jesus into the courtyard of the high priest, but Peter was standing outside at the gate. So the other disciple, who was known to the high priest, went out, spoke to the woman who guarded the gate, and brought Peter in. The woman said to Peter, "You are not also one of this man's disciples, are you?" He said, "I am not." Now the slaves and the police had made a charcoal fire because it was cold, and they were standing round it and warming themselves. Peter also was standing with them and warming himself.

Then the high priest questioned Jesus about his disciples and about his teaching.

Notice what you think and feel as you read the gospel.

Judas betrays Jesus. He leads the soldiers to Jesus to arrest him. The disciples scatter, as Jesus is led before Annas and Caiaphas. Outside the gate, Peter denies being a disciple of Jesus.

Pray as you are led for yourself and others.

"Lord, you were treated unjustly, and it has just begun. Help me not be unjust with others. I pray for those I have wronged . . ." (Continue in your own words.)

Listen to Jesus.

If you can be good and loving in any situation, even a situation that is cruel and unjust, you elevate that situation, make it meaningful, and redeem it. That is what I do. Follow me. What else is Jesus saying to you?

Ask God to show you how to live today.

"Then help me to be good and loving in all my circumstances today, and this will be a day of glory for you. Thank you. Amen."

Saturday, March 31, 2018
Holy Saturday

**Know that God is
present and ready to converse.**

"Crucified Savior, I know you live and are here with
me now. I praise you."

Read the gospel: Mark 16:1–7.

When the sabbath was over, Mary Magdalene, and
Mary the mother of James, and Salome bought spices,
so that they might go and anoint him. And very early
on the first day of the week, when the sun had risen,
they went to the tomb. They had been saying to one
another, "Who will roll away the stone for us from
the entrance to the tomb?" When they looked up, they
saw that the stone, which was very large, had already
been rolled back. As they entered the tomb, they saw a
young man, dressed in a white robe, sitting on the right
side; and they were alarmed. But he said to them, "Do
not be alarmed; you are looking for Jesus of Nazareth,
who was crucified. He has been raised; he is not here.
Look, there is the place they laid him. But go, tell his
disciples and Peter that he is going ahead of you to
Galilee; there you will see him, just as he told you."

**Notice what you think
and feel as you read the gospel.**

The women find the stone rolled away and the tomb
empty. A young man in a white robe tells them not to

be alarmed, for Jesus has been raised. He asks them to tell the others to go to Galilee, for there they will see Jesus.

Pray as you are led for yourself and others.

"Jesus, the events of your death and resurrection are straightforward and mysterious at the same time. The miraculous invades the mundane world. Let it be so in my life, too . . ." (Continue in your own words.)

Listen to Jesus.

I will grant your prayers as you ask. I am alive and I live for you. And you will live for me forever in the glorious kingdom of heaven, prepared for you by my Father from all time. What else is Jesus saying to you?

Ask God to show you how to live today.

"Then let me love you and serve you today, Lord. Let me do your will until you call me to yourself. Amen."

Sunday, April 1, 2018
Easter Sunday

Know that God is
present and ready to converse.

"You are always present with me, Lord, but sometimes I do not recognize you. Reveal yourself to me and teach me by your Word."

Read the gospel: John 20:1–9.

Early on the first day of the week, while it was still dark, Mary Magdalene came to the tomb and saw that the stone had been removed from the tomb. So she ran and went to Simon Peter and the other disciple, the one whom Jesus loved, and said to them, "They have taken the Lord out of the tomb, and we do not know where they have laid him." Then Peter and the other disciple set out and went toward the tomb. The two were running together, but the other disciple outran Peter and reached the tomb first. He bent down to look in and saw the linen wrappings lying there, but he did not go in. Then Simon Peter came, following him, and went into the tomb. He saw the linen wrappings lying there, and the cloth that had been on Jesus' head, not lying with the linen wrappings but rolled up in a place by itself. Then the other disciple, who reached the tomb first, also went in, and he saw and believed; for as yet they did not understand the scripture, that he must rise from the dead.

Notice what you think and feel as you read the gospel.

Mary Magdalene first discovers Jesus' tomb is empty. Peter and John run to see, and they find the tomb empty, as she reported. They begin to realize that Jesus has risen from the dead.

Pray as you are led for yourself and others.

"Lord, let my heart burn within me as I hear and read your holy scriptures. You are the Word of God, the Light that came into the darkness. Make me what you please. I wish to serve . . ." (Continue in your own words.)

Listen to Jesus.

I AM, and the universe was created by me, through me, and for me. I give meaning and glory to all that is. You can reach out to me, and I want you to, but you can only begin to approach me now. Seek me and I will draw you into myself, beloved. What else is Jesus saying to you?

Ask God to show you how to live today.

"You are too high for me, my God, but I aspire to know you. Let me continuously advance my knowledge of you, your goodness, and your glory. Amen."

The
SACRED
READING
Series

Inspired by the traditions of Ignatian spirituality, the Sacred Reading series by the Apostleship of Prayer—an international Jesuit prayer ministry—is a unique guide to the use of lectio divinia through a simple, six-step process that provides a prayerful and imaginative exploration of the daily gospel readings and helps readers look for application in their own lives.

Ignatian Spirituality for Every Season

Find next year's editions wherever books and eBooks are sold.
For more information, **visit avemariapress.com.**

The Apostleship of Prayer (The Pope's Worldwide Prayer Network) is an international pontifical prayer ministry served by the Jesuits that reaches more than 35 million members worldwide through its popular website, apostleshipofprayer.org, and through talks, conferences, publications, and retreats. The Apostleship's mission is to encourage Christians to make a daily offering of themselves to God in union with the Sacred Heart of Jesus.

Douglas Leonard, who compiles the Sacred Reading series, served as the executive director of the Apostleship of Prayer in the United States from 2006 to 2016. He earned a bachelor's degree in English in 1976, a master's degree in English in 1977, and a PhD in English in 1981, all from the University of Wisconsin-Madison. Leonard also has served in higher education, professional development, publishing, and instructional design as an executive, writer, editor, educator, and consultant.